THE MYSTERIES OF LIGHT

The Mysteries of Light

THE NEW ROSARY
AS GOSPEL PRAYER

Wilfrid J. Harrington OP

DOMINICAN PUBLICATIONS

First published (2003) by
Dominican Publications
42 Parnell Square
Dublin 1

ISBN 1-871552-87-7

British Library Cataloguing in Publications Data.
A catalogue record for this book is available
from the British Library.

Cover design by Bill Bolger

Printed in Ireland by
The Leinster Leader Ltd
Naas, Co. Kildare.

Acknowledgements
Scripture quotations are from the New Revised Standard Version
Bible copyright © 1989, by the Division of Christian Educationof
the National Council of Churches of Christ inthe USA, and are
used by permission. All rights reserved.

For
Joan and Michael Glazier

Contents

Introduction   9

Gospel   12

Jesus   21

The Mysteries of Light

1. Baptism   31

2. Cana   49

3. Kingdom   59

4. Transfiguration   88

5. Supper   98

Conclusion   119

Introduction

Close to thirty years ago, in a book on the Rosary, [1] I stressed the firm Gospel basis of this traditional prayer. The Rosary is, indeed, a thoroughly biblical, a wholly Gospel prayer. The reason it is so is by no means only because the Lord's Prayer and the greater part of the Hail Mary come straight from the Gospels. It is because almost all of the 'mysteries' of the Rosary come straight from the Gospels. The Joyful Mysteries are taken from the first two chapters of Luke's gospel – his infancy narrative. The Sorrowful Mysteries are based on the passion narratives of the four gospels. The Glorious Mysteries reflect the close of the Gospel and its overflow into the new age of the Spirit and the Church.

A first matter to be cleared up is the meaning of the term 'mystery.' In common use, 'mystery' means hidden, not readily discernible – we speak of a detective-mystery. In older catechesis 'mystery' was defined as 'revealed truth which we cannot comprehend'. In biblical usage – and this is our guide here – *mysterion* is no longer 'mysterious'! A 'mystery' is a plan or purpose of God, hidden, true, in the past, but now revealed. Thus Paul, in Romans, writing of the destiny of Israel, declares: 'Brothers and sisters, I want you to understand this mystery: a hardening has come upon part of Israel, until the full number of the Gentiles has come in. And so all Israel will be saved' (11:25-26). Later writings speak of 'the mystery' long kept secret by God but now 'made manifest to his people' (Colossians 1:26). It emerges that the mys-

---

1. Wilfrid J. Harrington, *The Rosary: A Gospel Prayer* (Canfield, Ohio: Alba Books, 1975).

tery is identified with the person of Jesus Christ (Ephesians 3:4; Colossians 4:3; 1 Timothy 3:16) and, at the same time, is identical with the Gospel: the proclamation of the Gospel is the mystery that was kept secret for long ages, but now made known. In short, mystery is revelatory. The mysteries of the Rosary reveal Christ to us and lead us to further understanding of him.

The fifteen-decade Rosary, however, has a serious lack. The Joyful Mysteries reach only to the story of the twelve-year-old Jesus in the Temple. The Sorrowful Mysteries begin with Gethsemane. Not a trace of the Jesus of the ministry! And the fact is: it is not possible truly to understand the death of Jesus except in the context of his life. Jesus did not die – Jesus was killed. He was put to death precisely because of the witness he had borne, in all that he was and in all that he had said and done, throughout his ministry. 'Who do you say that I am?' is challenge of the Marcan Jesus (8:29). The answer is not in his death alone but in what led to his death. The proposed addition – more properly, insertion – by Pope John Paul II of Mysteries of Light [2] makes the Rosary a more balanced prayer.

It is striking that the Rosary, the Marian prayer par excellence, is taken up almost wholly with the Son of Mary. As the prayer is arranged she is, so to say, a frame to him. This remains so if the Mysteries of Light [3] find their natural setting between the Joyful and the Sorrowful Mysteries.

2. Apostolic Letter, *Rosarium Virginis Mariae*, 16 October, 2002
3. It seems to me that the 'official' title, The Luminous Mysteries, is more likely to hamper than to foster ready acceptance of the proposed addition to the Rosary. It does not ring pleasingly.

Mary does figure in the first two Joyful Mysteries, Annunciation and Visitation, while the last two Glorious Mysteries, Assumption and Queenship, are hers. In between, all is his. The emphasis is as it ought to be.

In the Mysteries of Light, Jesus is central. While the presentation of him reflects encounter with him as risen Lord, he is, firmly, Jesus of Nazareth. He is the one 'born of woman, born under the law' (Galatians 2:17), the 'one like his brothers and sisters in every respect' (Hebrews 2:17). It is this truth one would emphasise here. It is vitally important for a balanced teaching on the meaning of the life of Christ.

The Mysteries of Light come from the Gospels. It is, then, of concern to understand what is meant by Gospel and how Gospel is to be properly approached. The Mysteries have to do with episodes in the ministry of Jesus. An outline of that ministry, inasmuch as it is possible to trace its lines historically, will indicate the setting of the episodes. These concerns – Gospel and Jesus – are faced in our two opening chapters. Then the five Mysteries are taken in turn. Four of them – Baptism, Cana, Transfiguration, Supper – are precise episodes. The other – the Kingdom – is, in practice, the ministry of Jesus. The stress here is on salient aspects of the ministry. If Gospel texts are to be the basis of prayer – the meaning of the Rosary – one would wish to hear the texts aright. The modest aim of this book is to aid this hearing.

Gospel

These things are written that you may continue to believe
that Jesus is the Messiah, the Son of God,
and that through believing you may have life in his name.
(John 20:31).

Gospel is, on the whole, a distinctive literary form. Jewish and Hellenistic parallels of a sort there may be, but there is nothing quite like it outside of the New Testament. Our gospels are a mixture of narrative and discourse, centered on the person, life and teaching of Jesus of Nazareth, with special emphasis on his death and resurrection. All four evangelists are concerned to set out both the *story* of Jesus of Nazareth and also what they took to be the *significance* of his actions and teaching. He is the focus; he gives meaning to all.

A gospel is not objective biography. This story is shot through with resurrection faith. A gospel is written for believers: it is a Christian document addressed to Christians. More specifically, each of the gospels was, in the first place, written for a particular Christian community and with the needs of that community firmly in mind. The evangelists presented the 'facts' with the intention of bringing out the meaning which the events held for those who encountered them. They set out to voice the faith of the early Church. The nucleus of that faith is that the crucified Jesus had been raised from the dead.

The fourth evangelist has given us the aim of an evangelist. His selective presentation of the 'signs' of Jesus was in order that the Christian disciple might go on believing that the historical person, Jesus, is the Messiah of Jewish expectation, that he is Son of God. He wrote that, through their deepened faith in Jesus Christ, Christians might find life in him and live that life more fully (John 20:31). In other words, his concern was christology and discipleship. The gospels are proclamations of the Good News. They are aimed at Christians striving to live the Christian Way.

PLOT AND CHARACTERS

A gospel, addressed to a Christian community, has the concerns and needs of the community in mind. These are concerns and needs perceived by the evangelist (not necessarily by the recipients or not by all of them). His readers know the basic story as well as the author. He makes his point by telling the story in his manner. Each of the evangelists tells essentially the same story (manifestly true of Mark, Matthew and Luke, the Synoptists), but the emphases of the gospels differ considerably. The events and actions of a story, the plot, regularly involve conflict; indeed, conflict (not necessarily violent conflict) is the heart of most stories. Not alone do the gospels have plots but the plot is, in a sense, the evangelist's interpretation of the story. As writers of narrative literature, the evangelists achieved their purpose by means of plot and characterisation.

Characterisation refers to the manner in which a narrator brings characters to life in a story. In literary terms, 'characters' are not the same as persons. In day-to-day life we know one another imperfectly. I may guess at your thoughts; I cannot really know what you are thinking. Characters can be transparent. The narrator may fully expose a character to the readers, can permit the reader to get inside the character. Alternatively, one can present a 'true' picture of any character, or characters, make them known to us more intimately than they, as persons, were in fact known to their contemporaries.

The distinction between 'character' and 'person' is important. Jesus of Nazareth was a wholly historical person. He was a first-century Palestinian Jew who carried out what – he was convinced – was a God-given mission to his people. He was rejected, and was condemned and executed by an alliance of Jewish religious and Roman political authorities. The 'character' Jesus of the gospels is this Jesus now viewed through Christian eyes, seen through the prism of resurrection-faith. Each gospel has several characters, of varying importance for the flow of the story. Jesus is always the chief character; the evangelist speaks, primarily, through him. Jesus carries the central message of each gospel. And Jesus is chief spokesman of an evangelist's concern.

MARK

One may illustrate this play of plot and characterisation in terms of the gospel of Mark. This is appropriate because Mark's text will figure most prominently in our study of the Rosary Mysteries. As in story in general, the events and actions of the Marcan story involve conflict, and Jesus is the immediate source of the conflict. We glance, firstly, at conflicts between Jesus and the authorities, and then at those between Jesus and his disciples.

Jesus versus the authorities

The authorities involved were the religious and political leaders – and in relation to them Jesus was at a disadvantage. Mark does indeed show Jesus having facile authority over evil spirits – the exorcisms, and over nature – the stilling of the storm. But Jesus' authority does not extend to lording it over people. Still, what Jesus said and did challenged directly the authorities of Israel. For their part, the authorities viewed themselves as defenders of God's Law. They contended that Jesus assumed unwarranted authority for himself, interpreted the Law in a manner they considered illegal and disregarded many religious customs. They responded by proferring charges against him.

Jesus, for his part, had been anointed to usher in God's rule (Mark 1:9-11). The issue for him was how to get the authorities to 'see' God's authority in his actions and teaching. The narrator skilfully created tension and suspense. Already by the end of the five conflict stories (2:1–3:6) the sides are clearly established (3:6). The impending clash with the authorities is kept in sight throughout the journey to Jerusalem (8:27–10:52). The climactic confrontation in Jerusalem came quickly. It is noteworthy that the first accusation against Jesus was a charge of blasphemy: 'Why does this man speak in this way? It is blasphemy!' (2:7) – thus, from the start of the story, Jesus walks a tightrope. Nevertheless, the reader recognises that Jesus is firmly in control. At the trial he himself volunteered the evidence his accusers needed: ' "Are you the Messiah, the son of the Blessed One?" Jesus answered, "I am." ' (14:61-63). Jesus, not the authorities, determined his fate.

Jesus and the disciples

At stake in the conflict with the disciples is whether Jesus can make them good disciples. The disciples struggled at every point to follow Jesus but were simply overwhelmed both by him and by his demands. Jesus' efforts to lead the disciples to understand were matched by their fear and their hardness of heart. Theirs was not the determinmed opposition to Jesus of the authorities – they were trying to be his followers. They did consistently misunderstand Jesus' teaching and ended up by failing him utterly. Yet, they had followed him to Jerusalem. Jesus just could not get his chosen disciples (effectively the Twelve) to understand him, could not get them to do what he expected of them.

In an effort to bring them to realize how dense and blind they were, he hurled challenging questions at them (4:13,40; 8:17-21,33; 9:19; 14:37,41) – and was met with silence. He tried to prepare them for his impending death and for his absence. He knew that they would fail him in Jerusalem; yet he sought to urge them to stand by him (14:37, 41-42). The outer conflict reflects an inner conflict: they want to be loyal to Jesus, but not at the cost of giving up everything, least of all their lives.[4]

The fact remains that readers of the gospel are most likely to empathise with those same disciples. By doing so, the readers come to discern their own inadequacies. They find comfort in the realisation that, although the disciples failed him, Jesus remained unflinchingly faithful to them.

4.See D. Rhoads and D. Michie, *Mark as Story* (Philadelphia: Fortress, 1982).

A new beginning

Jesus did not manage to make them faithful disciples. They failed him – and the question stands: will they learn from their failure and, beyond his death, at last become truly followers of him?

When Jesus had warned his followers of their immminent failure (14:26-31) he had added a reassuring word: 'After I am raised up, I will go before you to Galilee.' (14:28). That word is then caught up in the message of the 'young man' at the tomb: 'Go, tell his disciples and Peter that he is going before you to Galilee; there you will see him, just as he told you' (16:7). Throughout the gospel, to 'see' Jesus means to have faith in him. What Mark is saying is that if the community is to 'see' Jesus, now the Risen One, it must become involved in the mission to the world that 'Galilee' signified. Galilee was the place of mission, the arena where Jesus' exorcisms and healings had broken the bonds of evil. There, too, the disciples had been called and commissioned to take up Jesus' proclamation of the coming rule of God. 'Galilee' is the place of universal mission. But no disciple is ready to proclaim the gospel until she or he has walked the way to Jerusalem (10:32-34) and encountered the reality of the cross (15:39).

THE FOURTH GOSPEL

The literary characteristics of Mark are found, too, broadly speaking, in Matthew and Luke. The Fourth Gospel – though it tells the same story – is notably, even startlingly, different. The structure of the Fourth Gospel as a whole is notably dramatic. This skilfulness of presentation is also present in the larger individual episodes within the gospel, such as the Samaritan woman (4:1-42), the cure of the blind man (9:1-41) and the raising of Lazarus (11:1-44). In these episodes the reader is brought stage by stage to a full revelation of Jesus. And the reader, too, comes to an increasing certainty of faith.

These longer narrative complexes illustrate the conflicts of opinion, the antagonism between belief and unbelief. At the same time these episodes serve to present the struggle between light and darkness, a struggle in which, looked at from the outside, the powers of darkness and unbelief appear to be gaining the upper hand. Even in shorter passages such as the marriage at Cana (2:1-11), the cleansing of the temple (2:13-22) and the healing of the official's son (4:46-54) dramatic presentation is not lacking. Here, too, one finds the moment of suspense before the liberating vision of faith.

An aspect of the dramatic in John is present in the emphasis placed on 'signs.' The signs are mighty works performed in sight of Jesus' disciples – miracles. Still, it is by contrasting 'miracle' and 'sign' that we can best understand John's intention. The restoring of sight to a blind man at Siloam (9:1-12) is indeed a miracle, quite like similar miracles in the Synoptics (see Mark 9:27-31). But John is not interested in this or other miracles as such; his interest is in their symbolism, their signification. For him, the restoring of sight to a blind man is a sign of the spiritual light which Christ, who is Light, can give, because he viewed the actions of Jesus as pointers to a deeper meaning.

We are not always left to work out these hidden meanings for ourselves because, in many cases, these are brought out in the discourses that accompany the signs. We are also thus provided with a criterion for judging other passages where such comment is lacking. The signs are closely linked to the work of Jesus on earth. Their purpose is to bring out the deeper dimension of his works, to reveal the glory of the Son.

John's theology

John has indicated, firmly, the purpose of his gospel: 'These [signs] are written so that you may continue to believe that Jesus is the Messiah, the Son of God, and that through believing you may have life in his name' (20:31). His intent is to bring people to believe, more profoundly, that the man of flesh and blood, Jesus of Nazareth, is the Messiah of Jewish expectation – and something far, far more than that. 'That you may continue to believe' looks to those who already believe – who have believed without seeing (20:29) – inviting them to a more profound and stable faith. This faith is directed to the living and glorified Lord, preached by the church, living in the church. He is the Saviour, the Lord of glory – and none other than the Jesus of the gospel. Faith in him has the power to bestow salvation, life 'in his name.' And there is the promise, and the challenge: 'Those who abide in me and I in them, bear much fruit, because apart from me you can do nothing' (15:5).

The Johannine world is characterised by division into light and darkness, life and death. This warfare between light and darkness is not cosmic but is a struggle within humans in a search for truth and life. In the Johannine view, truth has come, whole and entire, with the coming of the

Son. In him the meeting of God with humankind has taken place: he is the communication of divine life. The truth, light and life which humans need have been brought by the Son; they are given because he is one with humankind.

For John the story of Jesus is that place in history where the ultimate truth about God is to be found. More than the Synoptists it is he who gives us an awareness of this through his theme of life. John had more to tell about Jesus than any gospel could hold. He had glimpsed the divine light which all the while irradiated the Teacher from Nazareth.

The incarnation is a beginning. It has to be fulfilled in the work for which the Son had been sent into the world: the glorification – revelation – of the Father that in turn is the glorification/revelation of the Son. The 'hour' of Jesus, the hour of his suffering and death, is one phase of his 'glorification,' the other being his resurrection and going to the Father. Now he is revealed for who he really is.

In contrast to the Synoptists, John has underlined the 'glorification' aspect of the passion story. It is an hour of triumph because, despite appearances, it is the 'world' – unbelieving humankind – that stands judged, and the power of evil broken. The incarnate Word has revealed God by his words and deeds – and has himself been revealed. The 'hour' of Jesus is gradually unveiled throughout the Fourth Gospel in the various 'signs', beginning with Cana: 'the first of his signs.' The climactic hour is on the cross: 'When you have lifted up the Son of Man, then you will realize that I AM' (8:28). It is the hour of 'glorification', the hour of revelation of the Father. That is why Jesus died with the confident words: 'It is accomplished!' (19:30).

Jesus

*For we do not have a high priest who is unable
to sympathise with our weaknesses, but we have one
who in every respect has been tested as we are,
yet without sin ... Therefore he had to become
like his brothers and sisters in every respect.
(Hebrews 4:15; 1:17)*

The New Testament makes clear that, following on initial
varying perceptions of him, Christian faith came to focus
on the *risen* Jesus and on his vital presence among them as
Spirit. Christology – theological understanding of Jesus –
emerged and developed. It was never lost to sight that the
risen Lord and Jesus of Nazareth are one and the same.

IMAGE OF GOD

'God was in Christ, reconciling the world to himself' (2
Corinthians 5:19). This is, arguably, the very best statement
we have about Christ, and it weds teaching about Christ
with teaching about salvation: where Jesus is, there is God;
and God is there for us. But Jesus of Nazareth is the thoroughly human person who was 'born of woman' (Galatians
4:4), who lived in our world, who died, horribly, on a cross.
We meet God in Jesus. The author of Hebrews has told us
in no uncertain terms: 'Long ago God spoke to our ancestors in many and varioius ways by the prophets.' This is
revelation of God indeed, but fragmentary and mediated
through servants. 'In these last days he has spoken to us by
a Son ... he is the reflection of God's glory and the exact
imprint of God's very being'. (Hebrews 1:1-3)

If Jesus bears the stamp of God's very being he does so as a human person. Like us in all things, Jesus shows us what God is like. Jesus is God's summons to us, God's challenge to us. We can say, truly, that God is love; but we have no idea of what God's love is in itself. In Jesus we see God's love in action. We learn that God is a God who is with us in our suffering and in our death. We are sure of it because of the suffering and death of Jesus.

In Jesus, God has shown himself in human form: 'he is the image of the invisible God.' (Colossians 1:15). In practice we have slipped quickly past this human aspect. We have turned, instead, to a 'divine icon' comfortably free of any trait of the critical prophet. We have confined Jesus to his heavenly home. We have done so because Jesus of Nazareth is a very uncomfortable person to have around, a constant challenge. We look to this Jesus.

JESUS OF NAZARETH

The object of Christian faith is the person of Jesus Christ who once lived, briefly, in the first century A.D. and now lives on in the Father's presence. The real or actual Jesus is this glorified Saviour, alive in our midst. The gospels proclaim Jesus of Nazareth as the Christ, the definitive revelation of God. The proclamation, aimed at eliciting a faith response, embraces strictly historical elements (e.g. Jesus' death on a cross) and theological interpretation, interpretation which makes use of biblical categories (e.g. ascent to God's right hand).

The gospels present us with the 'earthly Jesus': a picture of Jesus during his life on earth. Their partial, and theologically coloured, pictures serve as the sources for gaining a picture of what we might call 'the historical Jesus.' We need to realise that not even the most sophisticated modern research can fully reconstruct a historical figure. But to attempt such reconstruction is of immense importance – particularly in our day. Jesus is an appealing and a challenging figure.

Theology, the study of faith, if it is to be credible and effective, must reflect the culture within which it takes shape. Modern theological thinking about Christ, then, has to take cognisance of todays's concern about history and has to accommodate the quest for the historical Jesus. While there is material in the gospel narratives that is not historical in the modern sense, the gospel picture is 'accurate' – not in the sense that it is exact in detail but that it is truth-bearing. It is the acceptance of it by the early believing community that guarantees the substantial truth of the gospel account.

The gospel Jesus is more than the historical Jesus: the gospel presents not only history but the transhistorical, not only fact but theological interpretation. On the other hand, the ecclesiastical proclamation of the Jesus-image is often less than, is unfaithful to, the historical Jesus in which the image is rooted. This is a further reason for investigating into the historical Jesus. We must not shrink from facing up to the 'dangerous memory' of an often nonconformist Jesus, the challenge of his life and demands.

The Hisotrical Jesus

Jesus of Nazareth was a first-century A.D. Jew who began, lived and ended his short life in Palestine, a minor province of the Roman Empire. Our information about him, by historical standards, is meagre. Apart from two brief state-ments, by the Jewish historian Flavius Josephus and the Roman historian Tacitus respectively, our sources for knowl-edge of the historical Jesus are the canonical gospels alone. We may list some of the salient facts.[5]

Around 7-4 B.C., that is, towards the close of the reign of Herod the Great, a Jewish boy, to be named Jesus (Yeshua), was born, either in Bethlehem of Judaea or Nazareth of Galilee. His mother was named Mary (Miryam), his puta-tive father Joseph (Yosef). He grew up in Nazareth and was known as 'the Nazarene.' His native language was Aramaic; he would have had a practical command of Greek. It is highly likely that he was literate; as a boy he would have been taught in the village synagogue. Like Joseph, Jesus was a *tekton*, an artisan – most likely a carpenter. In a small village, Joseph's would have been the only carpenter shop; the family would have had a frugally comfortable life-style. Jesus lived and worked in the quiet obscurity of that Galilean village until, in his early thirties, there came a radical change, one that eventually led to his death by crucifixion. We are unable to date precisely the birth, ministry and death of Jesus. What follows is a fair approximation:

BIRTH	7-6 B.C.
BEGINNING OF MINISTRY	28 A.D. If Jesus began his minis-try early in 28, it would have lasted a little over two years.
DEATH	30 A.D., 14 Nisan – eve of Passo-ver. Jesus would have been about thirty-six at his death.

5. See John P. Meier, *A Marginal Jew*. Vol I (New York: Doubleday, 1991)

DISCIPLE OF THE BAPTIST

The starting-point for any account of the ministry of Jesus of Nazareth is his encounter with John the Baptist: the call which Jesus heard when he was baptised by John and to which he responded. The Baptism narratives will be studied in some detail below – the first of these new Rosary Mysteries. By submitting to baptism Jesus became, in effect, a disciple of the Baptist.[6]

John had begun his mission in the wilderness (Luke 3:2) of Peraea beyond the Jordan, appearing where Elijah had disappeared (2 Kings 2) and forcing the question of his identity (Mark 1:6). A wilderness audience would be Galilean pilgrims – avoiding hostile Samaria in a roundabout way to Jerusalem (see Luke 9:51-53). Jesus, very likely, had heard of the eschatological prophet, herald of the End-time. Now, as a Galilean pilgrim, he encountered this strange and striking man, who wore a camel-hair cloak bound with a leather belt: an Elijah-figure. Jesus accepted baptism and stayed on with John – as Elisha had become a disciple of Elijah. Later, some of John's disciples, possibly at his instigation, transferred to Jesus (John 1:35-42).

Some statements in the Fourth Gospel imply much more than might appear at first sight. Take John 3:22-23 – 'After this Jesus and his disciples went into the Judean countryside, and he spent some time with them and baptised. John was also baptising at Aenon near Salim [in Samaria].' We could take this to mean that John had sent Jesus into Judaea while he had gone to the more challenging Samaria. That

6. Jerome Murphy-O'Connor, 'John the Baptist and Jesus: History and Hyptotheses,' *New Testament Studies* 36 (1990), 259-374.

the ministry of Jesus involved baptism is explicit in 3:22 and in 4:1 – 'Now when Jesus had heard, "Jesus is making and baptising more disciples than John … " ' The observation reflects a later dispute as to the relative merits of John's and Jesus' baptisms. It is obvious that 4:2 – 'although it was not Jesus himself but his disciples who baptised' – is a later editorial 'correction.' Evidently, the concern was to distance Jesus from the Baptist.

Later, John moved into Galilee, territory of Herod Antipas and was promptly arrested (he had earlier denounced Herod's adulterous affair with Herodias, Mark 6:17-18). The observation in John 4:3 is significant: '[Jesus] left Judaea and started back to Galilee.' The Baptist had been silenced. Jesus moved in to take his place: *noblesse oblige*.

What emerges from all this is that, at first, Jesus was disciple of, and in the line of, the Baptist. At some time there was a radical change.

The point seems to have been reached with Jesus' welcome for sinners. Although he admired John, Jesus was to follow his own way. John was a prophet of doom who preached 'a baptism of repentance for the forgiveness of sins' (Mark 1:4) – and we need to keep in mind that Jesus, too, baptised. On the other hand, Jesus proclaimed: 'The kingdom of God has come near' (1:15). It is a matter of emphasis. Where John's message was the judgment of God, Jesus' message was the salvation of God. Hearing, in prison, of the activity of Jesus, a perplexed John sent two of his disciples to investigate. Jesus' reply was: 'Go and tell John what you have seen and heard: the blind receive their sight, the lame walk, the lepers are cleansed, the deaf hear, the dead are raised, the poor have good news brought to them' (Luke 7:22). One can read between the lines. John was being told that there was another prophetic message, another prophetic style. One might put it that John was in the line of Amos – that prophet of unrelieved gloom. Jesus was in the line of Hosea – prophet of God's gracious love. We must not, however, overlook the fact that Jesus, like Hosea, also spoke words of warning.

The baptism of Jesus by John is certainly historical – note the embarassment of Matthew 3:13-15. We look to the implication of it. In the first place, it indicated a fundamental change in Jesus' life: he became a disciple of the Baptist. He had come to know the eschatological message of John and showed, by his adherence, his basic acceptance of it. He submitted to John's baptism as a seal on his decision to change his manner of life. Hitherto, he had been a village carpenter; henceforth he would be proclaimer of the word. He would preach *metanoia*, a radical change of heart, in a wholehearted striving to renew Israel. The baptism launched him on a road that would eventually lead to the cross – though, surely, this prospect did not then appear on his horizon. Aspects of his ministry will be subject of a later chapter (Kingdom).

FAILURE?

The ministry of Jesus ended in final conflict with religious and political authority. The truth of the matter is that his death marked Jesus as historically a failure. Jesus was executed on the order of a Roman provincial official: an alleged trouble-maker in that bothersome province of Judaea had been summarily dealt with. The incident did not raise a ripple in imperial affairs. Yet history has shown that this execution was an event of historic dimension. Its ripples flow stronger than ever two thousand years later.

Let us be clear about it. The Romans and the Jewish Sanhedrin had effectively closed the 'Jesus case'. The aims and message of Jesus had ended with his death. His prophetic voice had been muzzled. This is failure.

The question arises: Why had Jesus been silenced? It was because he, unflinchingly, had lived and preached God's love for humankind. That is why he had table fellowship with sinners, why he sought to free women and men from religious tyranny, why he, at every hand's turn, bore witness to the true God. He might, in face of threatening opposition, have packed it in and gone home to Nazareth. That would have been failure indeed. But he would not be turned from witnessing to God's love. They might take his life, but to his last breath he would witness. What Jesus tells us is that failure is not the last word. That is, as God views failure.

GOD-FORSAKEN

Jesus came to bear witness to a God bent on humankind. Now he entrusts his experience of failure to God. He, like us, had to reconcile a painful experience of failure with trust in God. The Synoptists show that in no way did Jesus begin his mission with a vision of violent death at the end of the road. And if, at a later date, he had to face the fact that death was the likely outcome, the Gethsemane episode shows that he had to struggle to understand God's way, and, bow, filially to the Father's will (Mark 14:32-42). His Gethsemane decision was to trust in God despite the darkness of his situation. This was his most severe testing.

Jesus entered, fully, into our human lot of suffering and death. It is, surely, comfort that he feared the prospect of an atrocious death. He had a painful feeling of failure: the bottom had fallen out of his world. He cried out, in consternation, to his God (Mark 15:34). In reality, this failure was his triumph. He was experiencing what Paul was to perceive: the scandal of the cross. The scandal is the infinite reach of the love of God: 'If God is with us, who is against us? He who did not withold his own Son, but gave him up for all of us, will he not with him also give us everything else?' (Romans 8:32)

VINDICATION

Throughout his ministry Jesus had preached the rule of God – God as salvation for humankind. His last, involuntary, sermon was the most eloquent of all. The close of his earthly pilgrimage was to be his unequivocal proclamation of true divinity and true humanity.

For the cross is God's revelation of himself. It is there he defines himself over against all human caricatures of him. Paul had seen to the heart of the matter: 'We proclaim Christ crucified, a stumbling block to Jews and foolishness to Gentiles, but to those who are called ... Christ the power of God and the wisdom of God. For God's foolishness is wiser than human wisdom, and God's weakness is stronger than human strength' (1 Corinthians 1:22-25). God, in the cross, is a radical challenge to our pride, our *hubris*. There he is seen to be the *Deus humanissimus* – the God bent wholly on the salvation of humankind.

The career of Jesus did not end on the cross. The resurrection is God's endorsement of the definition of both God and humankind made on the cross. Just as the death of Jesus cannot be detached from the life lived before it, his resurrection cannot be detached from his career and death. Because he was raised from the dead, Jesus holds decisive significance for us. Because of the fact of his resurrection we know that meaningless death – and, often, meaningless life – has meaning. Jesus died with the cry on his lips, 'My God, my God, why have you forsaken me?' The sequel was to show that God had not forsaken Jesus.

We have the assurance that he will never abandon us. While, unlike his immediate disciples, we do not follow him to Jerusalem, we do join his human pilgrimage from birth to death. His word of promise is that we shall follow him beyond death to share his rest (see Hebrews 12:2). We shall know fully our Abba at last and become wholly his children.

1 Baptism

'You are my Son, the Beloved;
with you I am well pleased.'
(Mark 1:11)

Mark 1:9-11

¹The beginning of the good news of Jesus Christ, the Son of God. ²As it is written in the prophet Isaiah, 'See, I am sending my messenger ahead of you, who will prepare your way; ³the voice of one crying in the wilderness: "Prepare the way of the Lord, make his paths straight."' ⁴John the baptizer appeared in the wilderness, proclaiming a baptism of repentance for the forgiveness of sins. ⁵And people from the whole Judean countryside were going out to him and were baptized by him in the river Jordan, confessing their sins. ⁶Now John was clothed with camel's hair, with a leather belt around his waist, and he ate locusts and wild honey. ⁷He proclaimed, 'The one who is more powerful than I is coming after me; I am not worthy to stoop down and untie the thong of his sandals. ⁸I have baptized you with water; but he will baptize you with the Holy Spirit.'

⁹In those days Jesus came from Nazareth of Galilee and was baptized by John in the Jordan. ¹⁰And just as he was coming up out of the water, he saw the heavens torn apart and the Spirit descending like a dove on him. ¹¹And a voice from heaven, 'You are my Son,

the Beloved; with you I am well pleased.'

Matthew 3:13-17

[13]Then Jesus came from Galilee to John at the Jordan, to be baptized by him. [14]John would have prevented him, saying, 'I need to be baptized by you, and do you come to me?' [15]But Jesus answered him, 'Let it be so now; for it is proper for us in this way to fulfil all righteousness.' Then he consented. [16]And when Jesus had been baptized, just as he came up from the water, suddenly the heavens were opened to him and he saw the Spirit of God descending like a dove and alighting on him. [17]And a voice from heaven said, 'This is my Son, the Beloved, with whom I am well pleased.'

Luke 3:21-22

[21]Now when all the people were baptized, and when Jesus also had been baptized and was praying, the heaven was opened, [22]and the Holy Spirit descended upon him in bodily form like a dove. And a voice came from heaven, 'You are my Son, the Beloved; with you I am well pleased.'

John 1:29-34

[29]The next day he [John] saw Jesus coming toward him and declared, 'Here is the Lamb of God who takes away the sin of the world! [30]This is he of whom I said, "After me comes a man who ranks ahead of me because he was before me". [31]I myself did not know

him; but I came baptizing with water for this reason, that he might be revealed to Israel.' ³²And John testified, 'I saw the Spirit descending from heaven like a dove, and it remained on him, ³³I myself did not know him, but the one who sent me to baptize with water said to me, "He on whom you see the Spirit descend and remain is the one who baptizes with the Holy Spirit." ³⁴And I myself have seen and have testified that this is the Son of God.'

MARK 1:9-11

John the Baptist had summoned people to a change of heart (Mark 1:4-5). Then he went on to make his solemn proclamation: 'The one who is more powerful than I is coming after me … ' (1:7). We await the appearance of the Coming One. And, straightway, Jesus came from Nazareth of Galilee to be baptised by John. The description of the baptism is matter of fact. There is no trace here of the embarrassment evident in Matthew's text (Matthew 3:14-15). Mark ignores the difficulty – a difficulty perceived by some – raised by the fact of Jesus submitting to John's baptism 'for the forgiveness of sins.' In this evangelist's eyes, Jesus is not only the true Israelite coming to baptism; he is the Son of God receiving the sign of repentance on behalf of the people of God. (See 2 Corinthians 5:21). Here the contrast between the 'all' of v. 5 (the people 'from the whole Judean countryside and all the people of Jerusalem' who came to be baptized by John) and the 'one' of v. 9 becomes acute. In Mark's Gospel Judaea and Jerusalem are implacably hostile, in contrast to Galilee, the land of Jesus. The 'all' did not really respond to the Baptist's summons; this Nazarene alone offered himself in true submission. Only in his case was a 'coming up' out of the water matched by a 'coming down' from heaven.

The Voice

According to Mark, at the baptism, Jesus alone saw and heard the heavenly happenings (1:10-11); the divine word was for him. 'He saw the heavens torn apart' – the tearing open of the heavens indicated a divine communication. 'The Spirit' is the power of God coming upon Jesus, the Son. It is consecration for his messianic mission: 'how God anointed Jesus of Nazareth with the Holy Spirit and with power' (Acts 10:38).

The phrase 'like a dove' – descending dove-like – is found in all three Synoptists. The dove symbolism likely has reference to the mission of Jesus; its precise meaning escapes us. Jesus heard a 'voice from heaven' reminiscent of the rabbinic *bath qol* (literally, 'daughter of a voice'), that is, echo of a heavenly voice. The declaration: 'You are my Son, the Beloved; with you I am well pleased' gathers up a number of Old Testament texts:

1. Psalm 2:7, 'you are my son' – the Davidic king is God's adopted son;
2. Genesis 22:2,16, 'your only (i.e. beloved) son' – Abraham's beloved son, Isaac;
3. Isaiah 42:1-2, in whom my soul delights' – God's suffering Servant.

This transaction between Father and Son is a secret beyond human experience and will remain unknown to the characters in the gospel. Yet it is revelation, for the reader knows who Jesus is. The baptism story, as we find it in Mark, was meant to assert that Jesus was constituted and declared Son of God at the time of his baptism by John. It is, obviously, of first importance to determine what the title 'Son of God' would have meant for Mark.

Son of God

The New Testament church confessed Jesus as Son of God and, in doing so, attributed to Jesus a unique relationship to God. The question then is: was the title Son of God bestowed on Jesus during his lifetime? The title was used, in association with the title Messiah, by the high priest (14:61) – but the passage between the high priest and Jesus (14:61-62) reflects the christology of the evangelist, his theological understanding of Jesus. The heavenly voice, at baptism and transfiguration, declaring Jesus to be 'my Son, the Beloved' (1:11; 9:7), states Mark's own christology and is for the sake of the reader. The confession of the centurion (15:39) at that moment in the gospel (immediately after the death of Jesus on the cross) is a firm christological statement. In short, Jesus had not, in fact, been addressed as Son of God during his ministry. As for Jesus himself, the one text in which he referred to himself absolutely as the Son ('about that day or hour no one knows, neither the angels in heaven, nor the Son, but only the Father', 13:22) implies his subordination to the Father. On the other hand, Jesus did address God in Aramaic as *Abba* (14:36). There is no evidence that, in Palestinian Judaism, *abba* was used in address to God. Jesus' usage is distinctive and suggests his consciousness of a unique relationship: he was, indeed, Son of the Father.

The Secret

The title Son of God is of major importance for Mark. The celebrated designation, 'Messianic Secret,' of Mark's practice of having Jesus, again and again, impose silence on the recipients of his healing or on those who seemed to suspect who he was, is a misnomer. The element of secrecy concerns not Jesus' role as Messiah, but his identity as Son of God. It follows that the titles 'Messiah', 'Son of Man', 'King,' bestowed on Jesus are not, in the evangelist's estimate, wholly adequate. Mark takes care to identify his own evaluative point of view with that of the protagonist of his story: Jesus. Consequently, there is only one correct way in which to view things: the way of Jesus, which is also Mark's own way.

The evangelist took a step further and made certain that both his assessment and that of Jesus were in accord with the point of view of God — hence the voice from heaven (1:11; 7:9). It follows that the perception of Jesus which is normative in Mark's story is God's perception. The title which God bestowed on Jesus is paramount.

The heading of the gospel — 'The beginning of the good news of Jesus Christ, the Son of God' (1:1) — already informs the reader of Mark's understanding of Jesus' identity. In the baptismal scene the heavenly voice (the voice of God) declared of Jesus; 'You are my Son, the Beloved' (1:11). As Jesus was about to embark on his public ministry, God solemnly affirmed both his status and his call. Similarly, at the transfiguration God declared (this time for the benefit of the three disciples): 'This is my Son, the Beloved: listen to him!' (9:7). Only at baptism and transfiguration does God emerge as 'actor' in the story. And not alone did God, each time, declare that Jesus was 'Son,' but the declaration served the purpose of confirmation. The baptism declaration confirmed the truth of the caption (1:10); the transfiguration declaration confirmed the truth of Peter's confession of Jesus as 'Messiah' (8:29) — going beyond Peter's misunderstanding (vv. 32-33). Finally, at the climactic moment of the death of Jesus the title was Son of God: 'Truly, this man was God's Son!' (15:39). The centurion was the first human in Mark's Gospel to penetrate the secret of Jesus' identity — because he was the first to come to terms with the cross.

As for the meaning of 'Son of God' — the words of the voice from heaven, we have observed, form a composite quotation: from Psalm 2:7; Genesis 22:2; Isaiah 42:1. In Isaiah 42:1 the servant in whom God delights is one 'chosen' for ministry; in Genesis 22:2 Abraham's beloved son is his 'only' son. Most importantly, in Psalm 2:7, 'you are my son' is declared by Yahweh of the Davidic king. Consequently, with these words, God solemnly affirms that Jesus, the Anointed One (Messiah-King) from the line of David, is his only or unique Son whom he has chosen for End-time ministry — leader of God's people with the mission of gathering them for the End-time kingdom. It is this same understanding of 'Son of God' we find in Matthew and Luke.

MATTHEW 3:13-17

That Jesus was baptised by John the Baptist is, surely, among the most certain historical facts in the Gospel tradition. This is underlined by the obvious embarrassment in Matthew's text. Here only in the Synoptic accounts does the Baptist recognize Jesus before the baptism. He tries to prevent Jesus from undergoing this baptism of repentance meant for sinners. Jesus appeals to God's plan of salvation. It befits John and him 'to fulfil all righteousness,' to conform to the roles mapped out for them. Matthew's text shows the Christian embarrassment (quite absent from Mark 1:9) that Jesus should have undergone a 'baptism of repentance for the forgiveness of sins' (see Mark 1:4) and at the hands of his inferior, John.

The voice of the Father is for all present (and not for Jesus only, as in Mark): Jesus is not being designated Son for the first time – he had been so declared in Matthew's infancy narrative (Matthew 1-2). Rather, his sonship is proclaimed to others: 'This is my beloved Son.' In Matthew's account the emphasis is on the revelation of Jesus as Son of God, not on the baptism as such.

Why had Jesus come to be baptised? To inaugurate his mission (and, in effect, the messianic age); to raise the baptism of John to a new level; to show his solidarity with sinful humankind; to give an example of humility. The vision (3:16) sets the seal of divine approval on this mission of Jesus.

LUKE 3:21-22

With his 'when Jesus also had been baptized' (3:21a) Luke has further distanced Jesus from John's baptism and has continued the trend by avoiding any suggestion of a special baptism of Jesus and by omitting the name of the Baptist. His own distinctive emphasis is on prayer: Jesus 'was praying.' He finds, too, special significance in the descent of the

Holy Spirit on Jesus (3:22). This is in keeping with his stress, throughout his Gospel and Acts, on the role of the Spirit.

JOHN 1:29-34

In the Fourth Gospel there is an obvious concern to distance the Baptist even further from Jesus: it is merely implied that John had baptised Jesus. In 1:19-28 is the Baptist's vehement negative testimony: he is not the Messiah! Nor is he Elijah — traditionally, on the basis of Malachi 3:1; 4:5, expected to precede the Messiah. And he is not the prophet-like-Moses, another traditional messianic precursor (see Deuteronomy 18:5,18). He is a voice, only a heraldic voice — and yet the solemn voice of the wilderness prophet of Isaiah 40. If he baptises it is with water — in contrast to the one who 'baptizes with the Holy Spirit' (1:33). John is no more than a slave whose task it is to untie his master's sandal, and he feels unworthy even of that. Not John himself but disciples of the Baptist who still claimed John as Messiah (see Acts 19:1-4), are being put in their place.

In John's presentation, the sole purpose of the Baptist was 'to testify to the light, so that all might believe through him' (1:7). He bore witness to Jesus as the Lamb of God and Son of God. He is 'the lamb of God who takes away the sin of the world' (v. 29). The operative phrase is 'of God': in biblical thought only God takes away or forgives sin (see Mark 2:7). With his 'lamb of God' the Baptist has in mind the Passover lamb (John 19:14). He may, too, be thinking of the Servant of the Lord who is compared to a lamb in Isaiah 53:7-12, For that matter, within the broader sacrificial system, a lamb figured regularly in rites of reconciliation and of communion after sin. More than likely, the evangelist had all of this rich background in view. In any event, Jesus is the one who will destroy the sin that envelops humankind, but he does so as the Lamb of God. He is the Son of God on whom the Spirit descended and rested – he has permanent possession of the Spirit (see Isaiah 11:2; 42:1). He will 'baptise' by sharing his Spirit. The evangelist knows that the glorified Jesus had bestowed the Spirit (John 19:30; 20:22).

The Testing

Mark 1:12-13
¹²And the Spirit immediately drove him out into the wilderness. ¹³He was in the wilderness forty days, tempted by Satan; and he was with the wild beasts; and the angels waited on him.

Matthew 4:1-11
¹Then Jesus was led by the Spirit into the wilderness to be tempted by the devil. ²He fasted forty days and forty nights, and afterwards he was famished. ³The tempter came up and said to him, 'If you are the Son of God, command these stones to become loaves of bread.' ⁴But he answered, 'It is written, "One does not live by bread alone, but by every word that comes from the mouth of God."' ⁵Then the devil took him to the holy city and placed him on the pinnacle of the temple, ⁶saying to him, 'If you are the Son of God, throw yourself down; for it is written, "He will com-

mand his angels concerning you," and "On their hands they will bear you up, so that you will not dash your foot against a stone.'" [7]Jesus said to him, 'Again it is written, "Do not put the Lord your God to the test."' [8]Again, the devil took him to a very high mountain and showed him all the kingdoms of the world and their splendour; [9]and he said to him, 'All these I will give you, if you will fall down and worship me.' [10]Jesus said to him, 'Away with you, Satan! for it is written, "Worship the Lord your God, and serve only him."' [11]Then the devil left him, and suddenly angels came and waited on him.

Luke 4:1-13

[1]Jesus, full of the Holy Spirit, returned from the Jordan and was led by the Spirit in the wilderness, [2]where for forty days he was tempted by the devil. He ate nothing at all during those days, and when they were over, he was famished. [3]The devil said to him, 'If you are the Son of God, command this stone to become a loaf of bread.' [4]Jesus answered him, 'It is written, "one does not live by bread alone."' [5]Then the devil led him up and showed him in an instant all the kingdoms of the world. [6]And the devil said to him, 'To you I will give their glory and all this authority; for it has been given over to me, and I give it to anyone I please. [7]If you, then, will worship me, it will all be yours.' [8]Jesus answered him. 'It is written, "Worship the Lord your God, and serve only him."' [9]Then the devil took him to Jerusalem, and placed

him on the pinnacle of the temple, saying to him, 'If you are the Son of God, throw yourself down from here, [10]for it is written, "He will command his angels concerning you, to protect you," [11]and "On their hands they will bear you up, so that you will not dash your foot against a stone."' [12]Jesus answered him, 'It is said, "Do not put the Lord your God to the test."' [13]When the devil had finished every test, he departed from him until an opportune time.

Jesus, baptised by John, began his ministry as disciple of the Baptist. He went on to launch his own distinctive mission. This was a major decision which involved other decisions. He was thoroughly convinced of his calling. He had, however, to work out for himself how his mission would be carried through; he had to learn how, perfectly, to represent the Father. To make the Abba known: that was his role. The temptation stories, placed, dramatically, by Matthew and Luke before the opening of his mission, incorporate decisions he has to arrive at throughout his ministry. In the Synoptics the link between baptism and testing is formal.

Each of the Synoptic Gospels shows Jesus subjected to temptation, to testing. Their wilderness testing accounts express in spiritual form a broadly based New Testament conviction that Jesus had to struggle to remain faithful to God's will.

Tested as we are

The Letter to the Hebrews tells us that Jesus was 'one who in every respect has been tested as we are, yet without sin'. (Hebrews 4:15) How are we to understand that 'without sin'? Is it a matter of being incapable of sin (*non posse peccare*)? Or is it being able not to sin (*posse non peccare*)? In the past, preference was for the former: Jesus was wholly incapable of sin. But this makes testing or temptation pointless. The author of Hebrews is quite sure that the testing was very real. Paul has the same view. This is brought out, splendidly, by C.H. Dodd in his comment on Romans 6:9-10 – 'death no longer has dominion over him [Christ]; the death he died, he died to sin once for all.'

> The sense of these words must be understood from other passages in which Paul speaks of the life and death of Jesus in relation to the condition of the world. Mankind was bound in the servitude of Sin, established in the 'flesh.' Thus the natural, flesh-and-blood life of man was the territory, so to speak, of Sin, and all dwellers on that territory Sin claimed as his own. Christ, by his incarnation, became a denizen of 'the flesh.' Sin put in its claim. In other words, Jesus was tempted to sin, as we all are tempted, in such forms as sin might take for one in his situation. But instead of yielding, and acknowledging Sin's dominion, as we all do, he rendered a perfect obedience to God ... 'and became obedient to the point of death' (Phil 2:8). Jesus, in plain terms, died rather than sin; and so his death, instead of being a sign of the victory of Sin over man's true nature, was a sign of the complete rout of Sin in a decisive engagement.[7]

Matthew and Luke also believe that Jesus was really tested – that he had to make moral decisions. Otherwise, their

7. *The Epistle of Paul to the Romans* (London: Collins, 1959), 106 f.

temptation story would be meaningless.

MARK 1:12-13

With the emergence of the beloved Son a new era had begun, the era of eschatological hope. An essential feature of this hope is the overthrow of evil – Satan. This Mark conveyed by adding the testing narrative (1:12-13) to his baptism narrative (vv. 9-11).

He had managed, too, a striking contrast in his presentation of the Forerunner and the Coming One. John is a man among crowds, preaching and baptising. With the appearance of Jesus we enter another world: the heavens torn open, the Spirit descending, a divine Voice, the Son of God, Satan tempting, and ministering angels.

Anointed with the Spirit for his task and confirmed in his sonship, Jesus faced a trial of strength. The Spirit 'drove' – a strong word – Jesus into the wilderness: recalling the place where Israel was 'tested' for forty years. In the context of the testing, a struggle with evil, the wilderness is the traditional haunt of evil spirits – symbolised by 'wild beasts'.

Jesus was tested – the word *peirazomenos* carries all the nuances of temptation, trial, tribulation, test. Testing is the appropriate rendering here. It evokes the testing of the suffering just person who, though tried by suffering, remains faithful and is called child of God (Wisdom 2:12-50; 5:1-23). For Jesus, testing did not end here (see Mark 14:32-42) and the implied victory over evil, reflected in his subsequent exorcisms, will have to be won all over again on the cross.

'Forty days' recalls Moses (Exodus 34:28) and the forty years of testing in the wilderness. It reminds us, too, of Elijah, who also received the ministration of angels (1 Kings 19:5-8). Here we are doubtless to understand that the ministering angels supplied Jesus with food; Mark has no reference at all to a fast of Jesus. At this first struggle Jesus is not God-forsaken as he feels to be at his last (15:34).

MATTHEW 4:1-11

At the start of this passage, Matthew shows Jesus experiencing what Israel had experienced in the desert – with the radical difference that this Son will conquer where God's son, Israel, had failed (Deuteronomy 8:2-5). The tempter immediately latched on to the question of Jesus' sonship. (It ought to be obvious that a literalist interpretation – and, *a fortiori*, presentation – of the 'temptations' must be avoided. This is a sophisticated piece of writing and one must correctly grasp Matthew's intent.) At the baptism Jesus had been solemnly acclaimed as God's Son (3:17); the question now is: how will he *function* as God's Son? One should keep in mind that Matthew is addressing his *Christian* community. In terms of this 'temptation' of the Lord he is reading them a salutary lesson.

'If you are the Son of God ...'

In each of his three ripostes to 'the devil' Jesus cited texts from Deuteronomy, and these texts are the key to the meaning of each scene.

1. 'One does not live by bread alone' (Deuteronomy 8:3). Jesus had been challenged to provide food miraculously for himself, to use his authority as Son apart from the Father's design.

2. 'Do not put the Lord your God to the test' (6:16). Again, Jesus was challenged to use his power on his own behalf, this time to dazzle his contemporaries and conform to *their* image of a heaven-sent messiah.

3. 'Worship the Lord your God and serve only him' (6:13). Jesus has been challenged to be wholly autonomous; to do things entirely his way. His firm decision is that if he is to have authority, *exousia*, he will have it from the Father alone. He will learn that his exercise of authority will ever be service, *diakonia*. Each time Jesus had prevailed by 'the sword of the Spirit, which is the word of God' (Ephesians 6:17).

To put the matter summarily: Jesus will not misuse his sonship to his own advantage; his disciple will not abuse his or her Christian status. In quoting Deuteronomy 8:3 Jesus had urged his trust in God, now he is challenged to turn that trust into crass presumption; the true Christian will not seek to put God to the test. Building on the promise that the Messiah-Son would have the nations for his inheritance (Psalm 2:6-8), the 'ruler of this world' (John 12:31; 16:11) presents himself as a god to be worshipped — only to be unceremoniously repudiated.

This bizarre episode is readily understandable when we observe that Jesus' reply is an emphatic assertion of God's fundamental command to Israel: monotheism (Deuteronomy 6:13). The Christian will, likewise, reject any form of idolatry — the idolatry of wealth, of ambition ...

LUKE 4:1-13

Luke's testing narrative is very close to that of Matthew 4:1-11 except that he has inverted the order of the second and third temptations. Matthew's sequence — stones into bread; pinnacle of the temple; high mountain — is more logical.

It cannot be doubted that Luke has changed the order so that the series might end at Jerusalem. This is in keeping with his theological interest in the city. His three scenes serve to correct a false understanding of Jesus' mission as Son. They depict him as Son of God, obedient to the Father's will, the faithful Son who will not be turned to invoking his authority for any other purpose than that for which he had been sent.

MEDIATOR

Jesus was 'tempted' in every respect as we, yet without sinning (Hebrews 4:15). A consistent biblical pattern, representing God's respect for humankind, is the role of mediator in God's dealing with people. Jesus was mediator (Hebrews 5:1-3; 8:6). In keeping with the reality of the human situation, God saw it fitting that the Son who leads men and women to salvation should be made perfect through suffering (2:10). Jesus learned from his suffering what obedience to God's will meant for humankind — 'and having been made perfect he became the source of eternal salvation for all who obey him' (5:9).

The temptations of Jesus are the ongoing temptations of Christians — to seek one's glory, even in religious matters; to seek the easy way and turn aside from suffering; to forget that the source of Christian life is to be found in the death and resurrection of Christ. Jesus redeemed humankind as the Suffering Servant and as Son of Man: by being one of us and in solidarity with his fellow men and women. We are redeemed by uniting ourselves with Christ. It is the way of countering the temptations that assail us.

2 Cana

'Do whatever he tells you'
(John 2:5)

John 2:1-12

¹On the third day there was a wedding in Cana of Galilee, and the mother of Jesus was there. ²Jesus and his disciples had also been invited to the wedding. ³When the wine gave out, the mother of Jesus said to him, 'They have no wine.' ⁴And Jesus said to her, 'Woman, what concern is that to you and to me? My hour has not yet come.' ⁵His mother said to the servants, 'Do whatever he tells you.' ⁶Now standing there were six stone water jars for the Jewish rites of purification, each holding twenty or thirty gallons. ⁷Jesus said to them, 'Fill the jars with water.' And they filled them up to the brim. ⁸He said to them, 'Now draw some out, and take it to the chief steward.' So they took it. ⁹When the steward tasted the water that had become wine, and did not know where it came from (though the servants who had drawn the water knew), the steward called the bridegroom ¹⁰and said to him, 'Everyone serves the good wine first, and then the inferior wine after the guests have become drunk. But you have kept the good wine until now.' ¹¹Jesus did this, the first of his signs, in Cana of Galilee, and revealed his glory; and his disciples believed in him.

In the Fourth Gospel the Cana story comes after the account of the first days of Jesus' ministry (1:19-51) and is an introduction to the response to Jesus within Israel (2:1-3:36).

It is significant that the wedding was on 'the third day' (2:1). This indicates that the background is Exodus 15 – the gift of Torah, the Law. More immediately, the background is the Jewish liturgical feast of Pentecost which developed from Exodus 19. 'The Lord said to Moses: Go to the people and consecrate them today and tomorrow ... On the morning of the third day ... Moses brought the people out of the camp to meet God' (Exodus 19:10,16-17). In the liturgical tradition these three days of Exodus were preceded by four days of more remote preparation – here reflected in John's four days (1:19-51). The 'third day' comes in 2:1-12, with the manifestation of the 'glory' of Jesus.

In the Prologue (1:1-18) John had established a contrast: 'a gift in place of a gift' (1:16). The gift that is truth, the authentic revelation of God in Jesus, perfects the gift formerly given through Moses: the revelation of God in Torah. The prologue of Hebrews offers an instructive parallel: 'Long ago God spoke to our ancestors in many and various ways by the prophets, but in these last days he has spoken to us by a Son' (Hebrews 1:1-2). John's 'third day' of Cana is the beginning of the manifestation of the greater gift.

The passage 2:1-12 is a careful construct, rich in the kind of symbolism typical of John. The first character in the story, the mother of Jesus, initiated the action with her implied request: 'They have no wine.' Jesus' response was abrupt: 'Woman, what concern is that to you and to me?' It draws a sharp line between Jesus and his mother. The second part of the response underlines this and suggests the reason: 'My hour has not yet come.' The 'hour' of Jesus which unfolds throughout the Gospel (see 2:4; 7:4, 30; 8:20) is at the pleasure of the Father. All the more surprising, after the rebuff, is the mother's reaction: 'His mother said to the servants, "Do whatever he tells you"' – enter the first believer, as in John's understanding of faith. Wholly unaware of her Son's role in God's design, she nevertheless demands that anything he asks should be done.

> She is the first person in the narrative to show, at the level of the action of the story, that the correct response to the person of Jesus is trust in his word... She trusts unconditionally, indeed even in face of apparent rejection and rebuke, in the efficacy of the word of Jesus.[8]

The water 'for the Jewish rites of purification' (v 6), turned into wine symbolises the old order yielding place to the new. For the evangelist, the episode is a symbol of something that occurs throughout the whole of Jesus' ministry – the manifestation of the 'glory' of Jesus, John's term for revelation. Revelation, in John, is self-revelation of Jesus – ultimately revelation of the Father. All the rest stems from this.

The significance of the wine here is that it is Jesus' gift, a sign which comes from him and points to him. As a gift of Jesus, the wine is, significantly, given towards the end of the narrative. So precious and copious, it is the eschatological gift of the Messiah. The evangelist is not referring to any particular gift (such as the Eucharist) but to Jesus himself as Revealer.

In the narrative the steward's remark that the good wine

8. Francis J. Moloney, *The Gospel of John*. Sacra Pagina 4. A Michael Glazier Book. (Collegeville, MN: The Liturgical Press, 1998), 68.

has been kept 'until now' (2:10) is, perhaps, ironical.

This 'now' of the remarkable gift of wine is but a first moment in the revelation of Jesus. And if at this, 'the first of his signs,' his disciples 'believe in him,' this was but a beginning. The full manifestation will not come until 'the hour'. The disciples have much, very much, to learn. At the 'hour' of consummation the mother of Jesus, woman of faith, will appear again (19:25-27).

The Cana story, thoroughly a composition by John, is wholly symbolic. We need to put the right question to it. In our Western culture, when we hear a story, our spontaneous reaction is, Is it true? — meaning, Did it really happen so? A Semite, hearing a story, asks: What does it mean? True, the Fourth Gospel was written in Greek, but its author was a Jew, a Semite. And the community of John was predominantly Jewish. The evangelist would have expected his hearers/readers to ask of this story: What does it mean? They asked the right question and got the right answer. It is indeed a story rich in John's theology. If we are to garner the riches of it we, also, must ask the right question.

It is worth observing that the liturgy of the feast of the Epiphany strings together the Magi story, the Baptism of Jesus and the Cana story:

Today the Church has been joined to her heavenly bridegroom, since Christ has purified her of her sins in the Jordan; the Magi hasten to the royal wedding and offer gifts; the wedding guests rejoice since Christ has changed water into wine. (*Benedictus* antiphon for Morning Prayer)

More strikingly:

> Three wonders mark this day we celebrate: today the
> star led the Magi to the manger; today water was changed
> into wine at the marriage feast; today Christ desired to
> be baptised by John in the river Jordan to bring us salva-
> tion. (*Magnificat* antiphon for Evening Prayer II)

The liturgy, too, displays exuberant imagination.

AT THE HOUR

[25] Meanwhile, standing near the cross of Jesus were
his mother, and his mother's sister, Mary the wife of
Clopas, and Mary Magdalene. [26] When Jesus saw his
mother and the disciple whom he loved standing beside her, he said to his mother, 'Woman, here is your
son.' [27] Then he said to the disciple, 'Here is your
mother.' And from that hour the disciple took her
into his own home. (John 19:25-27)

John has, by the cross of Jesus, the Mother and the Beloved Disciple. The mother of Jesus was the first person in
the story to trust unconditionally in the word of Jesus (2:3-5).
Now, 'lifted up' on the cross – his hour of 'glorification' –
Jesus bids her accept the Beloved Disciple as her son. He
bids that model disciple accept the Woman as his mother.
Jesus, at the moment of the 'hour,' had established a new
family.

Because of the cross and from the moment of the cross a
new family of Jesus has been created. The Mother of
Jesus, a model of faith, and the disciple whom Jesus loved

and held close to himself are one as the disciple accepts the Mother in an unconditional acceptance of the word of Jesus.[9]

At the 'hour' of Jesus the 'woman' of 2:4 had come into her own.

This scene at the cross is surely symbolic, as a new relationship is set up between the mother and the disciple. The disciple 'took her to his own home.' The model disciple obeyed unquestioningly the word of Jesus. But, historically, did anything of the sort happen? Mark tells us that at the crucifixion, 'There were also women looking on from a distance' (Mark 15:40; see Matthew 27:55; Luke 23:49), and makes no mention of the mother or of any male disciple. It is wholly unlikely that women and a male follower of the condemned Jesus would have been permitted to stand at the very site of execution. Like the Cana story, the episode at the foot of the cross is a theological statement by John. The question to be put to it is, emphatically, What does it mean?

JOHN'S PICTURE OF JESUS

Though the 'hour' of Jesus had not yet come at Cana, the episode is, by the evangelist, characterised as revelation of Jesus' glory. A sketch of the distinctively Johannine Jesus will serve to bring out the potential of that moment.

John's Theology

John has indicated, firmly, the purpose of his Gospel: 'These [signs] are written so that you may continue to be-

9. Francis J. Moloney, op. cit., 504.

lieve that Jesus is the Messiah, the Son of God, and that through believing you may have life in his name' (John 20:30). Obviously, he has sought to stress faith in the person of Jesus Christ and in his saving power. The foundation of that faith is his own presentation, his choice among the many signs which Jesus had wrought. His intent was to bring people to believe, more profoundly, that this man of flesh and blood, Jesus of Nazareth, is the Messiah of Jewish expectation – and something far, far more than that.

'That you may continue to believe' looks to those who already believed – who had believed without seeing (20:29) – inviting them to a more profound and stable faith. This faith is directed to the living and glorified Lord, preached by the church, living in the church. He is the Saviour, the Lord of glory – and none other than the Jesus of the gospel. Faith in him has power to bestow salvation, life 'in his name.'

Light and Darkness

John's world is characterised by division into light and darkness, life and death. This dualism has nothing to do with philosophical speculation on good and evil. This warfare between light and darkness is not cosmic but is a struggle within humans in a search for truth and life. In the Johannine view, truth has come, whole and entire, with the coming of the Son. In him, the meeting of God with humankind has taken place: he is the communication of divine life. The truth, the light and life which humankind needs, have been brought by the Son. They are given because he is one with humankind.

For John, the story of Jesus is that place in history where

the ultimate truth about God is to be found. The incarnation is a beginning. It has to be fulfilled in the work for which the Son had been sent into the world: the glorification – revelation – of the Father that in turn is the glorification/revelation of the Son. The 'hour' of Jesus, the hour of his suffering and death, is one phase of his 'glorification,' the other being his resurrection and going to the Father. Now he is revealed for who he really is.

In contrast to Mark, Matthew and Luke (the Synoptists), John has underlined the 'glorification' aspect of the passion story. It is an hour of triumph because, despite appearances, it is the 'world' – unbelieving humankind – that stands judged, and the power of evil that is broken. The incarnate Word has revealed God by his words and deeds and has himself been revealed.

The Johannine Jesus

In general, John and the Synoptists tell the same story, but tell it differently. While already in Matthew and Luke there is a tendency to stress what one might term the other-worldliness of Jesus, in John he seems something of a sojourner from another world.

In the synoptic gospels Jesus' message concerns the 'kingdom of God,' the benevolent rule of God. In John, what Jesus preaches, what he reveals, is himself. Jesus is still concerned to make the real God known, but now who God is can be found and seen in Jesus. True, it is in and through Jesus we come to know God, but John's emphasis is unique: 'No one has ever seen God; God's only Son, who is nearest to the Father's heart, has made him known' (1:18).

There is in John's Gospel a series of 'I am' sayings (e.g. 'I am the bread of life,' 6:35; see 10:11; 11:25...). This reaches its height in the four absolute 'I am' sayings (8:24, 28, 58; 13:19) – e.g. 'When you have lifted up the Son of Man, then you will realize that I AM' (8:28). Each time there is an echo of the divine name of Exodus 3:14 or, more immediately, of Isaiah 43:10-11. Jesus declares: I am the bearer of God's name and power.

We must not lose sight of the fact that throughout the Fourth Gospel, Jesus' subordination to the Father is just as clearly expressed (e.g. 5:19, 26).

The One Sent

For John, Jesus is the 'one sent.' He comes as agent of the Father, empowered to speak and act in the name of the Father. This role of agent explains otherwise contradictory statements in the Fourth Gospel. Tension is sharpest in the contrast of two declarations: 'The Father and I are one' (10:30); 'The Father is greater than I' (14:28). When we read them in light of the role of agent and against other texts throughout the gospel, we appreciate that there is no contradiction.

As shown to us by John, Jesus is always conscious of being the 'one sent'. His statements are unambiguous: 'I seek to do not my own will, but the will of him who sent me' (5:30). If he freely lays down his life it is because 'I have received this command from my Father' (10:18). He is Son, apprenticed to his Father; he has learned everything from his Father: 'The Son can do nothing on his own, but only what he sees the Father doing; for whatever the Father does, the Son does likewise' (5:19). 'The Father loves the Son and shows him all that he himself is doing' (5:20). It is precisely because he is agent, the fully empowered representative of the Father, that he is the living presence of that Father; he is endowed with the Father's name and power. 'Know and understand that the Father is in me and I in the Father' (12:38); 'Whoever has seen me has seen the Father' (14:9). He is God's Son because he is the one 'whom the Father has sanctified and sent into the world' (10:36).

Jesus speaks the I AM as the One who bears God's name and wields God's power. It is this 'glorification,' revelation of the Father, that Jesus began to manifest at Cana: 'Jesus did this, the first of his signs, in Cana of Galilee, and revealed his glory' (2:11).

3 Kingdom

'The Son of Man came not be served but to serve,
and to give his life as a ransom for many.'
(Mark 10:45)

At some point, Jesus of Nazareth, onetime disciple of John the Baptist, struck out on his own. According to the general run of the gospel narrative, he was engaged during the early stage of his ministry in three main types of activity:

– He was engaged upon a broad appeal to the public. His aim was to make people aware of the presence of God as an urgent reality and to invite their appropriate response. In this he echoed in some measure the clarion call of the Baptist.

– He set himself to minister to human need by healing the sick, exorcizing evil and awakening hope in those who had lost hope. And he sought to lead men and women into new life under the inspiration of personal attachment to himself. By going about doing good he gave concrete shape to his message of the rule of God – of ultimate salvation.

– While his ministry cast him, in part, as teacher, his outlook and approach differentiated him from rabbinic Judaism. He challenged people to rethink their ideas and hopes, only to be branded a heretic. He censured his contemporaries and, in particular, the religious authorities, for their misunderstanding of God's ways. In his ministry, controversy was forced upon him.

We shall look to some aspects of his ministry, in particular, to his roles of Prophet, Teacher and Healer, as he proclaimed, in word and deed, the Rule of God.

PROPHET

Jesus of Nazareth had responded to the challenge of an uncompromising prophet: John the Baptist. He became prophet in his turn and began to proclaim the good news of the rule of God. Soon, God would come in power, bringing about the Kingdom. But one did not wait, passively, for it to happen. There must he human openness and human response. Besides, the rule of God was already present – present in Jesus, in his words and deeds. It could not be otherwise: in Jesus God was present and active. Besides, he, as prophet, had been sent.

Renewing Israel

Jesus did not come proclaiming a 'new religion': he came to renew Israel. We shall see that his appointment of the Twelve was a prophetic declaration of just that. His call was for a radical change of heart, for *metanoia*. He had come to summon Israel to become what God had wanted his people to be. He had caught up the urgent call of the Baptist and made it his own. He was quite clear as to the range of his mission: 'I was sent only to the lost sheep of the house of Israel' (Matthew 15:24; see 10:5-6). Inherent in Jesus' vision, however, was a dimension that, eventually, would no longer fit in the old wineskins.

Jesus had a burning desire for the renewal of the people of Israel as God's holy elect. He would not define the holiness of God's people in cultic terms. He redefined it in terms of wholeness. Where other contemporary Jewish groups were, in their various ways, exclusive, the Jesus movement was inclusive. His challenge and his invitation were to all. What Jesus claimed was that the decisive intervention of God, expected for the end-time, was, in some sort, happening in his ministry. The kingdom is here and now present in history in that the power of evil is broken, sins are forgiven, sinners are gathered into God's friendship. The kingdom, though in its fulness still in the future, comes as a present offer, in actual gift, through the proclamation of the good news. But it arrives only on condition of the positive response of the hearer.

The Kingdom of God

The precise phrase 'kingdom of God' occurs only once in the Old Testament, in Wisdom 10:10. The expression was not current in Judaism at the time of Jesus and was not widely used by early Christians. 'Kingdom of God' is found predominantly in Matthew, Mark and Luke, the Synoptic Gospels, and then almost always on the lips of Jesus. It was evidently central to Jesus' proclamation.

> The kingdom of God was simply Jesus' special and somewhat abstract way of speaking of God himself coming in power to manifest his definitive rule in the end time. God's coming in power to rule in the end time: that is the point of Jesus' phraseology.[10]

And this is why 'reign' or 'rule' of God is a more satisfactory

10. John P. Meier, *A Marginal Jew*. Vol 2 (New York: Doubleday 1994), 414.

rendering of the Aramaic *malkutha di elaha*. 'Kingdom of God' is, however, traditionally firmly in place.

Jesus spoke, in the main, of a future kingdom. In the Lord's Prayer, he taught his disciples to pray that God's Kingdom would come — that God would come at the end to save his people (Matthew 6:10; Luke 11:2). In Matthew 8:11-12/Luke 13:28-29 Jesus spoke of many coming from east and west (Gentiles) to join Abraham, Isaac and Jacob at the glorious banquet in the kingdom of God. In Mark 14:25 (Luke 22:18) Jesus, in speaking of his imminent death, confidently saw himself at the table of that banquet — drinking new wine in the kingdom of God.

If asserting its future coming was dominant in Jesus' proclamation of the kingdom, there is evidence that he also spoke of the kingdom as, in some fashion, already present in his own words and deeds. We have, for instance, the Lucan sayings: 'If it is by the finger of God that I cast out demons, then the kingdom of God has come to you' (Luke 11:20; see Matthew 12:28); and 'the kingdom of God is among you' (Luke 17:21). There is, too, Mark 1:15: 'the kingdom of God has come near.' And Mark 2:18-20, on fasting, also intimates that in some manner the kingdom is already present: 'The wedding guests cannot fast while the bridegroom is with them, can they? As long as they have the bridegroom with them they cannot fast.'

When we have in mind the fact that the kingdom of God is not primarily a state or place but rather the dynamic event of God coming in power to rule his people Israel in the end-time, it is not surprising that the precise relationship between the future and the present of the kingdom is not specified. That is why Jesus can speak of the kingdom as both imminent and yet present. In Jesus' eyes his healings and exorcisms were part of the eschatologial drama that was already being played out and that God was about to bring to conclusion.

The important point is that Jesus deliberately chose to proclaim that the display of miraculous power throughout his ministry was a preliminary and partial realization of God's kingly rule. Indeed, the best way of understanding the nature of the kingdom, the rule of God, is by seeing it in action in the deeds and words of Jesus — in his very person.

Good News for the Poor

Jesus knew it to be his vocation to proclaim the true God, the Father. He knew that in faithfulness to his task he was making the kingdom present — in other words, he was proclaiming the coming of God as salvation for humankind.

How he saw his task is vividly portrayed in Luke's inroduction of Jesus' ministry (Luke 4:16-21). Coming to his Nazareth synagogue on a sabbath, Jesus was invited to take the Scripture reading. He opened the scroll of Isaiah and read out:

> The Spirit of the Lord is upon me,
> because he has anointed me to bring good news to the poor.
> He has sent me to proclaim release to the captives
> and recovery of sight to the blind,
> to let the oppressed go free,
> to proclaim the year of the Lord's favour. (Luke 4: 18-19)

He had taken care to close his reading before the next phrase of the Isaian passage – 'and the day of the vengeance of our God' (Isaiah 61:2). 'Vengeance' would be no part of his message – his programme of liberation theology. Then he declared: 'Today this scripture has been fulfilled in your hearing' (Luke 4:21).

In his programmatic statement Jesus pointed to the recipients of his good news: captives, blind, oppressed – all who are weakest and powerless. They are 'the poor.' The 'poor' are not only those with few or no possessions, and not only those whose poverty is 'spiritual.' In the biblical context the poor are the 'little people' who are incapable of standing up for themselves and hence, by reason of their need and sorry state, are God's protected ones.

The designation 'poor' (as in Luke's beatitudes for instance, Luke 6:20-26) is not idealization: the poor really do need help; the hungry stand in need of nourishment; the mourning are visibly sorrowing. All cry out for compassion. The 'poor' to whom Jesus announced the good news of the kingdom and whom he pronounced 'blessed', are not those whom he proposed as models of virtue but are persons literally 'down and out.' The kingdom of God, the consolation of the new age, is for the weak and the despised, for those who suffer, who weep, who sorrow.

Liberating God

In his message of the kingdom Jesus was aware, better than any other, that sin was the greatest evil, the ultimate slavery. He discerned sin in selfishness and greed, in the seeking of status – most reprehensibly in the seeking of ecclesiastical power and privilege. He was conscious of sinful structures, political and religious. Indeed, he turned authority upside down (Mark 10:42-45). He took his stand on the fatherhood/motherhood of God. He believed that all men and women are children of this Parent, that all are sisters and brothers. He regarded sin as whatever conflicts with that family relationship of respect and love. Logically, then, his prophetic message was 'good news for the poor.' The poor were victims of the oppressive power of sin, an oppression mediated through sinful structures. The concern of Old Testament prophets found urgency in Jesus' preaching.

In preaching the rule of God, Jesus was defining God. He proclaimed a God bent on the salvation of humankind. That is why he announced good news to the poor — the needy of every sort, the outcast. That is why he was friend of sinners, why he had table fellowship with them. And, in the long run, it was because Jesus had steadfastly proclaimed a God of overwhelming mercy that he ended up on a cross. Edward Schillebeeckx observes perceptively:

> What is particularly striking in Jesus' career is the essential relationship between the person of Jesus and his message of the approach of the kingdom of God. There is an inner connection between message and proclaimer, as there is an inner connection between the message and the action of Jesus which matches it. With his person, his message and his life-style Jesus stands guarantor for the liberating God who loves men and women. From Jesus' career it becomes clear to the believer that the God of Jesus, the God of Israel, accepts the whole person and

tries to renew him or her in the acceptance of relationship to themselves and others, in a world in which it is good for men an women to live. [11]

TEACHER

In Jesus, the roles of prophet and teacher overlapped – as they did, regularly, in the prophets of Israel. Jesus taught distinctively. And he taught with authority. As a first-century Palestinian Jew he, of course, shared much of the theology of his tradition. But there was more than enough in his teaching to set him apart. The ultimate factor was his understanding of God. Clashes with his religious opponents over matters of law, such as sabbath observance, were symptomatic of fundamental difference. Jesus knew full well that to proclaim one's belief in God is not enough. What matters, and matters utterly, is the kind of God in whom one believes. It makes, literally, a world of difference whether one's God is the true God or a distorted image of that God.

For Jesus, God is God of humankind. He is found where there is goodness and a striving for the liberation of humankind. We are human beings, created in the image of God; we are meant to image God. Our destiny is to be human – as God understands humanness. The corollary is that only with God can we reach full humanness. Jesus, with God, reached full humanness.

Mark has presented Jesus as Teacher and he gave an indication of the range of his teaching; Matthew and Luke have given much more than he of that teaching. One thing

11. Edward Schillebeeckx, *Jesus in Our Western Culture* (London: SCM, 1987), 275.

emerges, unmistakably. Jesus had an eschatological perspective indeed – but he was deeply concerned with life in the here and now. He sought to reform Israel: he desired the fabric of life in his day to be transformed.

Jesus had a refreshingly realistic understanding of salvation. Salvation happens in our world, in our history. Salvation comes from God but happens, as it must, in the lives of humans. It reaches into and touches every aspect of human life. Otherwise it would not be salvation of humankind.

Salvation is not confined within the limits of religion. Indeed, too often, religion has been and is an obstacle to salvation – the whole liberation of the wholly human. It is only where men and women are free to be truly human that the human person becomes the image of God. And it is only so that the true being of God may be revealed. Being image of God is not only the reflection of God but the revelation of God. The Marcan Jesus is, transparently, the one 'like his brothers and sisters in every respect' who is, at the same time, and in his sheer humanness, 'the reflection of God's glory and the exact imprint of God's very being' (Hebrews 2:17; 1:3).

Demanding Teacher

Jesus offers no soft option. Christians may be children of God but only on condition that they understand what this means and live what it demands. In particular, the demands of discipleship have been firmly traced: 'Anyone who wants to be a follower of mine must renounce self, take up one's cross and follow me' (Mark 8:34). Jesus delivered a challenge, the challenge of his own way as Son. Being a disciple is a serious business.

Yet, taking up one's cross is not at all to say that suffering is something that Christians should seek. Jesus did not seek suffering. Gethsemane is clear enough: 'Abba, Father, for you all things are possible; remove this cup from me.' (Mark 14:36) But, suffering will be part of Christian life as it was part of Jesus' life. The comfort is that the following can be in tiny steps. God is patient. His challenge is invitation. Faithfulness to one's way of life, concern for others in whatever manner, the caring gesture, the kind word – these add up. There will be heroes, the few; there will be those whose way will seem ordinary, drab – the many. Even in the things of God we are prone to measure by worldly standards. The Lord does not overlook the painful decision, the unspoken sorrow, the secret suffering. There are many more saints than those who may be honoured as such.

The authority of Jesus

It is clear from the gospels that Jesus had authority – *exousia* – from God. It is equally clear that this power of his did not have any shade of domination. Mark does indeed show Jesus having facile authority over evil spirits – the exorcisms – and over nature – the stilling of the tempest. But Jesus' authority did not extend to lording it over people.

For that matter, in relation to people, he was largely helpless. The hallmark of his authority in relation to people was consistently and emphatically that of service: *diakonia*. If Jesus did serve others, it was always from a position of strength. He would not do what others wanted him to do unless it be consonant with God's will. He would lead, but he would not control. He healed, both physically and spiritually, looking for nothing else than openness to his healing touch. He was friend of sinners – and we must not allow ourselves subconsciously to think that they were repentant sinners before he was their friend. No, he brfriended them in their brokenness.

Jesus certainly confronted the religious authorities but without seeking to impose his authority on them. He was content to hold the mirror up to them, urging them to discern in their attitude and conduct a betrayal of God's rule. But that was the measure of it. Response was their responsibility.

Jesus sought no advantage from his authority. He laid claim to no title – it was up to others to identify him. In his healing ministry Jesus became the man who relieved suffering. At the end he was the vulnerable one who became victim of suffering. He was, after all, the one who had come 'to serve, and to give his life as a ransom for many' (Mark 10:45).

In short, Jesus, in his authority as in all else, mirrored God. For God, the God of infinite power, is never a God of force. The Son never did, nor ever would, resort to force.

HEALER

In the modern world many find it difficult to accomodate the notion of miracle; many reject the possibility of miracle. In contrast, in the Graeco-Roman world of Jesus' day, miracles were quite willingly acknowledged. If Jesus did perform miracles they would readily be accepted as such by his contemporaries. The question is: did he, in fact, perform miracles? The gospel evidence is, firmly, that Jesus did perform startling deeds regarded by himself and others as miracles. Among these were, assuredly, deeds of healing.

Jesus' reputation as healer is emphatically attested by all four evangelists. This healing activity covered a range of afflictions: paralysis, blindness, leprosy, deafness and other ailments. His healings were not only motivated by his concern for sufferers, his sympathy with the afflicted. They were also a sign of the inbreak of the kingdom. The saving power of God was making its way into the lives of men and women.

Suffering

Here a cautionary word. Both in Christian theology and in Christian worship suffering had receded into the background. It is stressed that Jesus Christ's work of salvation has to do with forgiveness of sin and eternal life. There is much less concern with the gospel witness to Jesus' total sensitivity toward human suffering. The result is that the 'sufferings of this world' are regarded as of little importance. Sin is what really matters. The believing Christian will not complain but will 'offer up' one's sufferings. This is something that Jesus did not do – think of Gethsemane and the cry from the cross. (Mark 14:33-36; 15:34)

Indeed one may get the impression that though Jesus of Nazareth cared for those who suffered and pitied those who mourned, the risen Lord is preoccupied solely with sin. Claus Westermann has put it aptly:

> There is no passage in the Gospel which suggests that Jesus saw his task to be one of convincing the sufferer that one must bear suffering patiently. There are narratives in which Jesus combines the forgiveness of sins with

healing, but there are no narratives in which Jesus puts the forgiveness of sins in place of healing. [12]

Jesus never declared to a sufferer: I forgive your sins – but offer up your sufferings!

Exorcisms

Prominent among Jesus' miraculous deeds – especially so in Mark – were exorcisms. This aspect of Jesus' activity can and does upset our modern sensibility. In the world of Jesus, on the other hand, exorcism was readily accepted both in paganism and in Judaism.

The exorcisms of Jesus were, in fact, healings. The difference between them and the recognized healings is that in the exorcism the then current view that human ills were due to evil forces that warred against us, was more pronounced. And in them, too, the apocalyptic dimension was more present.

Here, more than elsewhere, we face the fact that Jesus of Nazareth was, authentically, a first-century Jew. When the author of Hebrews declared that Jesus 'had to become like his brothers and sisters in every respect' (2:17) he really meant it. Every human is influenced by his or her culture. We are people of our age, no matter how well we may come to understand people of other times. We cannot turn the historical Jesus into a citizen of the twenty-first century. While Jesus the healer was manifestly concerned with human suffering, his ultimate concern was with the deadly sickness of sin.

12. *Prayer and Lament in the Psalms* (Edinburgh: T. & T. Clark, 1981), 275.

FRIEND OF SINNERS

The parables of Luke 15 which deal with the reprieve of sinners are Jesus' answer to the 'scandal' of the Pharisees: 'All the tax collectors and sinners were coming to Jesus to listen to him. And the Pharisees and the scribes were grumbling and saying, "This fellow welcomes sinners and eats with them"' (15:1-2).

These parables reveal God's compassion for sinners, not as a timeless, general truth but as realised in the ministry of Jesus. The lost sheep is dearer to this Shepherd, this Jesus, precisely because it is lost! The parables demonstrate that the words and actions of Jesus are inseparable. He is not a teacher of morals outlining principles of conduct. Instead, his attitude towards, and his daily life with, the poor are the model of our behaviour. He has fulfilled perfectly – as he no doubt inspired – the words of counsel given later to his followers: 'Little children, let us love, not in word or speech, but in truth and in action' (1 John 3:18).

'I have come to call not the righteous but sinners' (Matthew 9:13). The declaration is not only a scandal to the 'righteous' – it is hope for sinners. The sinners are thereby promised that God will intervene and that his doing so involves the remission of debts (as illustrated by the parables of the Two Debtors, the Unmerciful Servant, and the Prodigal Son – Luke 7:41-43; Matthew 18:23-35; Luke 15:11-32). Though Jesus only seldom promised 'forgiveness of sins' in as many words, the subjects of God's mercy and forgiveness were ever present in the rich picture language of his parables and sayings. The 'little ones' and the 'poor' are indeed privileged, but the privilege is not in themselves but solely in the heart of God – his generous benevolence, his *eudokia*. Jesus does not promise the poor and the humble a 'reward' for their way of life, but a share in the favour which God grants to what is little, weak and despised.

Sinners

If we are truly to appreciate the scandal of the righteous at Jesus' befriending of sinners, we must understand who the sinners are.

The term 'sinners' in the Old Testament refers to people who, in some fundamental way, stand outside the Law. A representative text is Psalm 10 where the 'wicked' (*reshaim*) are described as follows: 'In the pride of their countenance the wicked say, "God will not seek it out;" all their thoughts are. "There is no God;" They seize the poor ... the helpless fall by their might ... They think in their heart, "God has forgotten, he has hidden his face, he will never see it."' (Ps 10:4.10-11). The Septuagint (the Greek Bible), rendered *reshaim* by 'sinners' (*hamartoloi*) and Greek-speaking Jews used the term of the non-observant who had thereby placed themselves outside the covenant. The 'sinners' of the Gospels are those non-observant by the standard of the 'righteous' and, by them, regarded as living blatantly outside the Law. Jesus counted such within his fellowship. This was conduct that genuinely caused serious offence. [13]

Lost Sheep, Lost Coin (Luke 15:3-10)

The Pharisees had set the Torah as the way of righteousness and had found in meticulous observance of it the

13. See E.P. Sanders, *The Historical Figure of Jesus* (London: Penguin Books, 1995), 226-237.

achievement of righteousness. All who did not know the Law, or who did not keep it, were 'sinners,' strangers to the way of righteousness. 'But this crowd, which does not know the law – they are accursed' (John 7:49). Jesus staunchly refused to categorise people; to him no one was outcast. The Pharisees could not bear that Jesus welcomed 'sinners' and sought them out.

Worst of all, and there is a note of disgust, if not a note of horror: he 'eats with them' (see 5:30; 7:34). It was axiomatic that one could not have communion with 'sinners': contact with these outcasts rendered one ritually unclean. What right had this Jesus to flout so basic a requirement of the 'tradition of the elders,' the broader Torah?

Jesus countered their accusation by telling three parables: the Lost Sheep, the Lost Coin, the Lost Son. His defence was that he sought and welcomed the outcast because such is the Father's will. God is vindicator of the poor; the faithful Son was vindicator in turn.

The outcasts, too, had caught the message. All their life thay had been told that they stood beyond the pale. They were without hope, robbed of hope by the 'righteous.' Here one might observe that only an infinitely gracious God can forgive the devastation visited by the 'righteous' on 'sinners,' in particular by 'righteous' with pastoral responsibility, throughout Christian history.

The plight of the 'outcasts' is well documented in the Pharisee and the Tax Collector (Luke 18:10-14). 'The tax collector, standing far off, would not even look up to heaven, but was beating his breast and saying, "God, be merciful to me, a sinner!" ' At the end of all, he could not really bring himself to accept that God was as the 'righteous' had painted him. At least, he dared to hope that he was not so.

Now, such as he were given glowing hope. This man of God, unlike the righteous, did not shun them. No wonder that 'sinners' flocked to Jesus. And he, insultingly branded 'friend of sinners,' would have accepted the designation as the truest compliment. His meat was to do the will of him who sent him (John 4:34). Nothing was dearer to the Father's heart than this loving concern for the outcast

Jesus was aware that he was acting as God would do. He translates God's actions for men and women. The parables tell of the one lost sheep, a lost coin, a lost son. To fellow-Jews who are irritated at his dealings with impure people Jesus wants to make clear through his action that God turns to lost and vulnerable men and women: Jesus acts as God acts. So he embodies a claim that in his actions and words God himself is present. To act as Jesus does, is to live out the reality of the kingdom of God and to show what the kingdom of God is: salvation for men and women. [14]

One who has such an appreciation of Jesus' perception of his mission will dare ask: 'What would Jesus do?' – and dare to act accordingly.

The Lost Son

Jesus' story of the Lost Son (Luke 15:11-32) is allegory; the characters are God, the sinner and the righteous. Jesus' purpose was not only to depict God's gracious forgiveness. It was to hold the mirror up to his critics. It was to challenge them to see themselves in the elder son. Jesus' parable

14. Edward Schillebeeckx, *op. cit.*, 20.

is a defence of his conduct, his concern for the 'little ones' whom the Pharisees had written off as outcasts. Defence, yes – yet profoundly challenging.

Jesus' Jewish hearers would have grasped the pathos of the young man's plight. What they would have found disconcerting was the wholly unexpected conduct of the father. To welcome back, without a word of reproof and without any condition at all, one who had shown himself so weak and untrustworthy, was incredibly foolish. They would have identified, readily, with the hardnosed other son – indeed, they were he! Yet, the fact that the story itself manifestly extolled the conduct of the father would have given pause. What is it all about? It is too much for humankind, as the second part of the parable brings out.

The elder son is, recognisably, the 'scribe and the Pharisee.' He was quite upset when he learned that the unexpected feast was to celebrate his erring brother's return. Again the father 'goes out' – his love reaches to all. But the elder son was indignant at the injustice of the situation. He did not say 'Father' as the other had. He spoke of 'working like a slave' and of 'obeying your command.' The younger son had been prepared to settle for servanthood. The other had the mentality of a 'hired hand,' the mind of a slave. That is why he could not understand the father's love, why he was shocked by that display of forgiving love. He had disowned his brother who is 'this son of yours'. He was, however, gently reminded that the returned one was 'this brother of yours'. And he was assured: 'you are always with me, and all that is mine is yours' – he was still the heir. His brother's return offered no threat.

Begrudgers

This story was Jesus' answer to the 'grumblers' – the begrudgers. He told them that God is supremely concerned with those whom they had branded and spurned as outcasts. He told them that he shared the concern of his Father: 'I have come not to call the righteous but sinners' (Mark 2:17).

In Luke's setting, the story is even more provocative. Luke's 'sinners' and 'Pharisees' are Christians. He was exercised by the intolerance of 'righteous' Christians. For them, God's mercy to sinners was scandal: it is not fair! And if, indeed, God is one to be served, if he is one who has set firm rules that are to be obeyed, then it is unfair that one would be saved without obeying the rules and without rendering service. That God should be more concerned with the wayward ones than with his faithful servants is intolerable. Many Christians would empathise with the elder son. Any who do so, whether they are aware of it or not, share his image of God. It is not Jesus' understanding of the Father.

A Father's Love

The truth is that those for whom God is loving Parent will not be resentful, because they understand the crazy logic of love. They, as brothers and sisters, will share the Father's yearning for the homecoming of the lost ones. They will enter gladly into the rejoicing. They know that this Father's love is inexhaustible, know that they will not be loved less because the Father's love embraces others – *all* others! They will love the Father for his generosity. Every gesture of forgiveness will remind them of the forgiveness they had received, of the love lavished upon them. They will understand that Jesus had sought out sinners precisely because he had known the Father's love. They will seek to enter more deeply into that love, they will want to rejoice at that generosity.

We have, unhappily, tended to imagine divine forgiveness in terms of a human model. Indeed, consistent with our, too often, flawed image of God, we assume that such forgiveness is reluctant: an offended deity is ready to forgive provided he gets his pound of flesh. It is a sad travesty of God's forgiveness, yet one that is prevalent.

Our Parent forgives, eagerly, wholly, if we give him the chance. 'I will get up and go to my Father': a turning to him is all he asks. He — and he alone — can and will do the rest. To seek God's forgiveness is a homecoming; to be forgiven is to be welcomed home. It is a joyous moment, to be savoured and celebrated. It is redolent of the rule of God.

PRAYER

Prayer is a Christian need. We are children of God and should turn, with childlike directness, to our Parent. In this world we are sisters and brothers of the Brother who walked his way to Calvary. The Christian way, lived beforehand by Jesus, so firmly proposed by him and by his earliest disciples, is a way that challenges us. It is a way we do not walk alone. But we are not alone, for he is with us. We meet him in our prayer and keep step with him on the way. He has taught us to pray to the Father, and we have learned to pray to him.

Prayer of Jesus

'Descended from David according to the flesh' (Romans 1:3), Jesus was a son of Israel. As a committed Israelite he was by definition, a man of prayer. Aside from Luke, who had a special interest in prayer, the evangelists do not elaborate on Jesus' prayer life. That is not surprising. Simply, they, like him, took prayer for granted. The realization that Jesus was a man of prayer may give us food for thought.

Mark, with charming candour, tells us that Jesus' addiction to prayer was something of a trial to his disciples. The evangelist has given a sample day in the early Galilean ministry, at Capernaum (Mark 1:21-34), a day of enthusiastic reception and of great promise. His disciples, caught up in the excitement, were chagrined when Jesus went missing (v. 37) – 'In the morning, while it was still very dark, he got up and went out to a deserted place, and there he prayed' (1:35).

Typically, Mark has said much in few words. Jesus had slept (he 'got up'), had snatched a few hours of sleep. For his mission he needed deeper refreshment, a more potent source of energy, and he found it in prayer to his *Abba*.

As one 'like us in every respect' (Hebrews 2:17), Jesus was wholly dependent on this God. He turned, spontaneously, to an Abba who would support him, who would back him in his endeavours. True, he was sent, one who had to plough his own furrow. But he was not alone because the Father was with him. The prayer of Jesus, his whole prayerful trust in his Abba, is an essential ingredient of any meaningful christology. And it is an incentive to us in our prayer.

Example

Prayer of and by Jesus, by example and not by contrived

design, is meant to alert the disciple to his and her dependence on God. If the Son found a need and a joy in converse with his Father, he could expect that the other children of God, his sisters and brothers, would, too, experience that need and that happiness.

The comforting fact is that Jesus, as our high priest, has not ended his prayer. Now with the Father, he has no need, any more, to pray for himself. Henceforth, he is the high priest who prays *for us*, who makes intercession for us, without respite (Hebrews 7:25).

Being convinced of the companionship of God was the secret of Jesus' own prayer life. What was it that moved him to mark his prayer with the new, intimate mode of address: *Abba*? It was his abiding sense of communion with the Father, his knowing he was never alone. That which Jesus felt with his Father was the same companionship his disciples, and all Christians, came to feel with him.

This is movingly conveyed in the Emmaus narrative wherein Cleopas and his companion had the comfort of his fellowship when 'Jesus himself came near and went with them' – when he, unknown to them, walked along beside them and then 'went in to stay with them' at eventide (Luke 14:13-35). There, as they broke bread together, they came to recognize their Lord, the one whom they had been given as their Friend. They had opened their door to him, and he came in to sup with them, and they with him (see Revelation 3:20). He vanished from their sight, but their eyes had been opened – to know that he was with them always, and that this itself would be their prayer.

FOLLOWERS

Jesus did not play an isolated role. The Gospels speak of those who *followed* Jesus. Always it is the verbal form 'to follow' (*akoloutheo*) – but we may reasonably speak of 'followers.' His ability to attract crowds continued to his last days. Indeed, this factor would have contributed to his execution: the authorities feared that he might spark unrest. See Mark 14:1-2.

Disciples

The word 'disciple/disciples' (*mathetes/mathetai*) proliferates in all four Gospels. In Acts it is used in reference to Christian disciples but this meaning is absent from the rest of the New Testament. We may take it, then, that, in practice, 'disciple' refers to the group of committed disciples that Jesus had gathered around himself. In the Gospels three traits of discipleship are evident:

1. Jesus took the initiative in calling people to follow him (e.g. Mark 1:16-20).
2. 'Following' Jesus meant literal, physical following, and involved leaving one's home, parents and livelihood (e.g. Mark 1:16-20).
3. Jesus warned his disciples that they might face suffering and hostility. See the sayings on saving and losing one's life (Mark 8:35 parr.) and on denying oneself and taking up one's cross (Mark 8:34 parr).

In short, Jesus' demand was radical: disciples were called to wholehearted commitment to himself and to his mission.

This demand of total commitment might seem to suggest exclusivity. Instead, it was the practice of Jesus and his disciples to hold open table fellowship with outsiders, even with the despised toll-collectors and sinners. To break bread with them was an eloquent expression of acceptance and friendship.

We see, then, an interesting configuration: (1) Jesus' disciples are marked by obedience to his peremptory call, denial of self, and exposure to hostility and danger; these three traits constitute the radical, stringent life of Jesus' disciples. (2) Yet this radical group, marked by these three traits, is taught to be radically open to others, even to those 'outside the pale.' [15]

Jesus, in deed as well as word, was demonstrating that his mission was to *all* Israel.

Women disciples
Mark tells of women at the crucifixion of Jesus:

[40] There were also women looking on from a distance, among them were Mary Magdalene, and Mary the mother of James the younger and of Joses, and Salome. [41] These used to follow him and provided for him while he was in Galilee; and there were many other women who had come up with him to Jerusalem. (Mark 15:40-41. See Luke 8:1-3; John 19:25)

The evidence is clear that some women did follow Jesus during his ministry in Galilee and accompanied him on his last journey to Jerusalem. It is not conceivable, especially in light of Jesus' stringent discipleship demands, that this could have happened without his active approval. There is the

15. John P. Meier. *A Marginal Jew*. Vol. 3 (New York: Doubleday, 2001), 72 f.

fact, however, that these women are never named 'disciples'. But, then, there was no word in Hebrew or Aramaic for female disciple. The Greek Gospels reflect that fact. We might put the situation like this: Though the historical Jesus did not have women disciples specifically *named* disciples, the women who followed him were, in reality, disciples.

Besides disciples who left all to follow Jesus physically, there were men and women who, without leaving their homes, supported Jesus and his followers. So, Lazarus (John 12:1-2), Zacchaeus (Luke 19:1-10), Martha and Mary (Luke 10: 38-42), the host of the Last Supper (Mark 14:13-15). There surely would have been others. It is reasonable to suppose that those healed by Jesus, as well as their families, would have been eager to support Jesus and his followers as well as they could.

The Twelve

All four Gospels attest that, from among his disciples, Jesus chose a core group – the Twelve (Mark 6:7, and parallel passages.; John 6:67). For one thing, chosen 'to be with him' (Mark 3:14), the Twelve exemplified most clearly what being a disciple meant. Their key role, however, was symbolic.

The central message of Jesus was that God was coming in power to gather and rule over all Israel in the end time. This was a widely expressed hope of post-exilic Judaism: the regathering of Israel, all twelve tribes.

It is within this overarching hope for the regathering in the end time of *all* Israel, all twelve tribes, that Jesus' choice of an inner circle of twelve disciples must be understood … The mere fact that Jesus the eschatological prophet chose to select twelve Israelite men from among his disciples to form a special group would, in the eyes of his adherents, set in motion the regathering of the twelve tribes, even before the twelve men actually did anything. [16]

And it is in light of the Twelve's symbolic significance that one can best understand the brief mission of the Twelve to Israel during Jesus' public ministry (Mark 6:6-13, and parallels). The sending was a symbolic prophetic gesture: it symbolised the process of regathering the scattered people of God.

The Twelve as such played no role in the early church. They are not mentioned in the New Testament after Acts 6:2. As individuals only Peter and, to a much lesser extent, the sons of Zebedee, John and James, emerge with any clarity. It was seemingly understood that their *raison d'etre* was their symbolic role in the eschatological mission of Jesus.

The Christian mission was carried out by *apostles* – those 'sent out' (*apostellein*) from and by Christian communities. The passage (Acts 13:1-4) on the designation and sending out by the Antioch community of Barnabas and Saul, is an eloquent instance of this.

Paul came to evaluate his apostolic role as a personal divine call: 'Paul an apostle – sent neither by human commission nor from human authorities – but through Jesus Christ and God the Father, who raised him from the dead' (Galatians 1:1).

16. John P. Meier, *op. cit.*, 153.

THE CROSS

These apostles – Christian missionaries – had done their work and Christian communities flourished. Mark's Christians were followers of Jesus who believed that he is Christ and Son of God. Yet, they had much to learn.

The evangelist set out to declare who Jesus is, to spell out the nature of his messiahship. It is easy enough, he realized, to declare, even with conviction: You are the Messiah. What matters is how one understands that confession. It does not ask too much of one to be willing disciple of a risen Lord. We, all of us, find triumph and glory congenial. Mark takes an uncompromising stand. Jesus is, of course, Messiah and Son of God; he is one who will come, without fail, to gather his elect (Mark 13:26-27). But he is, too, the suffering Son of Man who walked a lone path to his death, who died, as it seemed to him, abandoned even by God (15:39).

At first sight, a suffering Son of Man, painfully vulnerable, and a Son of Man radiant in divine glory (see Mark 14:62), seem contradictory. In actual terms of the Jesus story there is no contradiction. In Luke, the message was spelled out for the Emmaus disciples: 'Was it not necessary that the Messiah should suffer these things and then enter into his glory' (Luke 24:26). For Jesus, glory followed on suffering. It is the insight of the John of Revelation: the Victim is the Victor. Glory beyond suffering is a concrete expression of the truth that authority (*exousia*) is most authentically present in service (*diakonia*).

This is borne out by the two 'earthly' Son of Man sayings: the Son of Man with authority to forgive sins, and the

Son of Man, Lord of the sabbath (Mark 2:10, 28). Here is where, with urgency, the Son of Man is to be sought and found. [17] Jesus, friend of sinners, mirrors a God of forgiveness. Jesus put people before observance. It was precisely because of his commitment to people, precisely because he was perceived as friend of sinners, that Jesus suffered the torture of the cross. It was precisely because of his commitment that God exalted him.

When, among those who profess to be his followers, *exousia* is not *diakonia*, when forgiveness is not prodigal, the Son of Man is not being proclaimed. The suffering Son of Man, rejected friend of sinners, must be embraced and confessed before any who claim to be his disciples can proclaim the Son of Man of glory. Mark is wholly consistent.

17. The title, 'the Son of Man,' occurs more than eighty times in the Gospels and, practically without exception, as a self-designation by Jesus. Jesus, however, never set out the meaning of the phrase; nor was it ever used to identify him. In gospel usage it has become a title of Jesus. The expression itself is Semitic – a literal rendering of an Aramaic idiom (which means simply 'man'). The background of the title in the Gospels is, ultimately, Daniel 7. There, in an apocalyptic setting, one 'like a son of man' (a human being), came into the presence of God and was granted dominion and kingdom (Dan 7:13-14). It seems that Jesus, reflecting on Daniel and other Old Testament passages, had seized on that 'one like a son of man,' to whom God had given glory and dominion and had interpreted it as 'the Son of Man,' the specific human figure through whom God would manifest his victory. He would have seen himself as this instrument of God's plan. There are three types of Son of Man sayings in the gospels:

1. Those which refer to the earthly activity of the Son of Man (Mk 2:10,28).
2. Those which refer to the suffering of the Son of Man (e.g. Mk 8:31).
3. Those which refer to the future glory of the Son of Man (e.g. Mk 14:62).

In the long run, what is incomprehensible is the rejection and execution of the promised Messiah who would establish the rule of God, of the Son of God who would reveal the Father.

The originality of Jesus flows from the contrast between his heavenly authority and power and the humiliation of his crucifixion. Jesus, from the first, was indeed the Messiah, and yet had to receive from the Father, through the abasement of the cross, the title of Messiah. The meaning of his life is that, as Son of God sent by the Father, he had come to deliver men and women from all their enemies, from foes within and foes without. He came to forgive sins, not to chastise sinners. He came, but he will not impose. When it came to the test, rather than force the human heart, he humbled himself and permitted himself to be taken and shamed and put to death. In his faithful service of men and women he was manifesting and establishing the Rule of God.

4 Transfiguration

'This is my Son, the Beloved; listen to him.'
(Mark 9:7)

Mark 9:1-8

¹And he said to them, 'Truly I tell you, there are some standing here who will not taste death until they see that the kingdom of God has come with power.' ²Six days later, Jesus took with him Peter and James and John, and led them up a high mountain apart, by themselves. And he was transfigured before them. ³And his clothes became dazzling white, such as no one on earth could bleach them. ⁴And there appeared to them Elijah with Moses, who were talking with Jesus. ⁵Then Peter said to Jesus, 'Rabbi, it is good for us to be here; let us make three dwellings, one for you, one for Moses, and one for Elijah.' ⁶He did not know what to say, for they were terrified. ⁷Then a cloud overshadowed them, and from the cloud there came a voice. 'This is my Son, the Beloved; listen to him!' ⁸Suddenly when they looked around, they saw no one with them any more, but only Jesus.

Matthew 17:1-8

¹Six days later, Jesus took with him Peter and James and his brother John and led them up a high mountain, by themselves. ²And he was transfigured before them, and his face shone like the sun, and his clothes became dazzling white. ³Sdudenly there appeared to them Moses and Elijah, talking with him. ⁴Then Pe-

ter said to Jesus. 'Lord, it is good for us to be
you wish, I will make three dwellings here, one for
you, one for Moses, and one for Elijah.' ⁵While he
was still speaking, suddenly a bright cloud overshadowed them, and from the cloud a voice said. 'This is
my Son, the Beloved; with him I am well pleased;
listen to him!' ⁶When the disciples heard this, they
fell to the ground and were overcome by fear. ⁷But
Jesus came and touched them, saying, 'Get up and
do not be afraid.' ⁸And when they looked up, they
saw no one except Jesus himself alone.

Luke 9:28-36

²⁸Now about eight days after these sayings Jesus
took with him Peter and James and John, and went
up on the mountain to pray. ²⁹And while he was praying, the appearance of his face changed, and his clothes
became dazzling white. ³⁰Suddenly they saw two men,
Moses and Elijah, talking to him. ³¹They appeared in
glory and were speaking of his departure, which he
was about to accomplish at Jerusalem. ³²Now Peter
and his companions wre weighed down with sleep;
but since they had stayed awake, they saw his glory
and the two men who stood with him. ³³Just as they
were leaving him, Peter said to Jesus, 'Master, it is
good for us to be here; let us make three dwellings,
one for you, one for Moses, and one for Elijah' – not
knowing what he said. ³⁴While he was saying this, a
cloud came and overshadowed them; and they were
terrified as they entered the cloud. ³⁵Then from the

cloud came a voice that said, 'This is my Son, my Chosen; listen to him!' [36]When the voice had spoken, Jesus was found alone. And they kept silent and in those days told no one any of the things they had seen.

2 Peter 1:16-18

[16]For we did not follow cleverly devised myths when we made known to you the power and coming of our Lord Jesus Christ, but we had been eyewitnesses of his majesty. [17]For he received honour and glory from God the Father when that voice was conveyed to him by the Majestic Glory, saying, 'This is my Son, my Beloved, with whom I am well pleased.' [18]We ourselves heard this voice from heaven, while we were with him on the holy mountain.

In Mark the transfiguration episode ranks with the baptism (1:9-11) and Gethsemane (14:32-42) narratives and shows similarities with both. While it is no longer possible to say what transpired upon the mountain – Was it vision? Was it profound religious experience? – we must seek to understand what the episode meant for Mark. It certainly was important for him.

The saying of 9:1, on the kingdom coming with power, is the proper introduction to the transfiguration narrative. A feature of the coming kingdom will be the glorious advent of the Son of Man (see 13:24-17); the transfiguration was, in some sort, a preview of it: a dramatic promise of fulfilment. In light of this pointer, those 'standing here' are

Peter, James and John. The episode may be viewed as a 'christophany' – a revelation of who Jesus really is. Significantly, Matthew has characterised it as 'vision' (Matthew 17:9). The disciples have a preview of the glory that will belong to Jesus in the fulness of God's kingdom.

GLIMPSE OF GLORY

'After six days' (Mark 9:2) – outside the passion narrative no other temporal statement in Mark is so precise. It is remarkable that Luke (9:28), although he qualifies the statement ('about eight days'), is careful to preserve the reference. Evidently, in the tradition, there was a close connection between the event of Caesarea Philippi – Peter's confession (Mark 8:27-30; Luke 9:18-21) – and the episode of the transfiguration. The presence of the three disciples, Peter, James and John, underlines unmistakably the importance of the episode for Mark (see 5:37; 13:3; 14:33). The phrase 'apart by themselves' (v. 2) emphasises the revelatory character of the event. It is closely connected with the strict imposition of silence in v. 9.

The transfiguration (9:2), involving a change in Jesus' form, would, for the evangelist, be an anticipated glimpse of his glorified state. Dazzling white garments reflect the glory of their wearer (see Revelation 3:4; 7:9). In Romans 12:2 and 2 Corinthians 3:18 the verb 'to be transfigured' is used of the 'transformation' of the believer into the spiritual likeness of Christ. A transfiguration of the just in the world to come is an apocalyptic theme (Daniel 12:3; 2 Baruch 51:3-10; see 1 Corinthians 15:40-44; 2 Corinthians 3:18). The transfiguration is an anticipation of the resurrection glory of Jesus.

In Mark 9:4 the order Elijah and Moses (Moses and Elijah is the traditional order) is unusual. This may simply be because Mark will go on to speak of the second Elijah (the Baptist, vv. 11-13). 'Talking with Jesus' (v 4): Luke gives the theme of the conversation – the 'departure' (literally, the *exodos* or death) of Jesus at Jerusalem.

PRAYER

Luke's narrative (Luke 9:28-32) may be a pointer to the nature of the original happening. In the entire first part of Luke's text Jesus held centre stage. He went up a mountain, site of divine manifestation. He became absorbed in prayer and in the immediacy of communion with God his countenance was altered and his raiment shone with heavenly brightness.

'Two men' (Moses and Elijah) appeared to him and spoke with him of his 'departure.' This *exodos* is the imminent death of Jesus at Jerusalem (see Wis 3:2; 7:6; 2 Pet 1:15). Jesus' 'departure' or 'passing over' includes death, resurrection and entry into glory.

The term also, with the naming of Moses, evokes the Exodus. Jesus is being presented as the new Moses who would reveal to the new people of God not the Torah of old but the definitive revelation of God. Moses and Elijah stand for Law and Prophets, the Scripture of Israel. Jesus had come to perfect that Old Testament revelation (see Hebrews 1:1-3). Later, the risen Lord will open the minds of the Emmaus disciples 'to understand the scriptures,' that is, everything written about him in 'the law of Moses, the prophets and the psalms' (Luke 24:44-45).

What seems to be is that, on the mountain, Jesus himself, through prayerful meditation on the scriptures, in an ineffable mystical experience, came to understand that his destiny was to suffer and die.

Jesus, however, is not alone on the mountain: he has with him Peter and James and John. They do not share in the revelation but, as witnesses of his anticipated glory, they will be stronger to support the humiliation of the cross. In the event, they were wholly devastated by the death of Jesus. It may be that, when they did encounter the risen Lord, recollection of this transfiguration episode had helped their new understanding of that death.

REVELATION

In Mark, however, the Lucan aspect of revelation to Jesus yields wholly to the theme of revelation granted to the disciples. And now the entire first part of the narrative prepares for this. Jesus led the three disciples 'up a high mountain' where he was transfigured 'before them' (Mark 9:2). Elijah and Moses appeared 'to them' and it was for the disciples' benefit that the heavenly voice was heard, speaking of Jesus in the third person (9:7).

'It is good for us to be here' (Mark 9:5) — that is to say, this is a happy moment which ought to be prolonged. 'Dwellings' or 'tents' suggest the booths made of interlaced branches at the joyous feast of Tabernacles. But since Tabernacles had taken on an eschatological significance (Hosea 12:9; Zechariah 14:16-19; Revelation 21:1-3), these 'dwellings' evoke the heavenly dwelling-places of the blessed. The three 'dwellings,' one each for Jesus, Elijah and Moses, would have put all three on an equal footing. Peter really 'did not know what to say;' he has, yet again, totally misunderstood. The voice from heaven will set the matter straight: the Son alone speaks the full word of God. The cloud which now over-shadows them is the cloud of God's *shekinah* (the 'presence' or 'dwelling' of God), symbol of divine presence (see Exodus 40:34-38).

'This is my Son, the Beloved': in contrast to 1:11 (the baptism), the words are here addressed to the disciples (instead of to Jesus): they hear the divine approbation of Jesus as messianic Son.

'Listen to him' – the Beloved Son is also the prophet-like-Moses (Deuteronomy 18:15-19) whose teaching must be heeded. Fittingly, Elijah and Moses had disappeared and Jesus stood alone.

ELIJAH

⁹ As they were coming down the mountain, he ordered them to tell no one about what they had seen, until after the Son of Man had risen from the dead. ¹⁰ So they kept the matter to themselves, questioning what this rising from the dead could mean. ¹¹ Then they asked him, 'Why do the scribes say that Elijah must come first?' ¹² He said to them, 'Elijah is indeed coming first to restore all things. How then is it written about the Son of Man, that he is to go through many sufferings and be treated with contempt? ¹³ But I tell you that Elijah has come, and they did to him whatever they pleased, as it is written about him.'

The Elijah-passage (Mark 9:11-13), closely linked to the transfiguration episode ('as they were coming down the mountain'), is an answer to a difficulty that faced the early church. Christians claimed that Jesus was the Messiah. But Jewish tradition, based on Malachi 3:2-5; 4:5-6, held that Elijah's return would precede 'the great and terrible day of the Lord.' Implied in Mark's text (9:11) is a denial that Elijah had come. Jesus answered that the tradition about Elijah was based on Scripture.

The second part of the reply (9:12b-13) faced up to another objection: the Christian claim that John the Baptist was the promised Elijah-figure was disproved by the well-known fate of the Baptist. The reply is in terms of Baptist-Elijah typology. The Baptist's fate was prophetic of the fate of the Messiah. 'As it is written of him' (see 1 Kings 19:2,10): John 'had found his Jezebel in Herodias' (see Mark 6:17-28). It was fitting that the forerunner should, beforehand, walk the way the Son of Man must walk – a point made explicitly in Matthew 17:12. The Christian retort to the Jewish objection was that John was the perfect Elijah to the Messiah who had come.

ONLY THROUGH PRAYER

The healing of the epileptic boy (Mark 9:14-19) is also linked to the transfiguration story. While Jesus and the three were on the mountain, the remaining disciples had got involved in what must have been, for them, an embarrassing argumentation with learned scribes. Besides, a man had brought to them his epileptic son and they had failed to heal the boy. After Jesus had healed him, and he was alone with his disciples 'in a house,' they questioned him 'privately.' This Marcan technique, highlighting an private message for the disciples, is the evangelist's special address to his community. Jesus explained why the disciples had been unable to cope: prayer was vitally necessary because the healer must rely wholly on the power of God – 'This kind can come out only through prayer' (v. 29). Some manuscripts add 'and fasting.' The addition is understandable but wrong-headed – it misses the point of the story. Fasting would introduce something of one's own effort, while the point being stressed is total reliance on the Lord.

Also, in the story, the motif of faith is firmly stressed. Jesus upbraided the faithless generation. All – scribes and Pharisees, the people, the very disciples – have been without understanding and were hardhearted. And the boy's father had doubted the power of Jesus: 'If you are able' (vv. 22-23). He was told that faith does not set limits to the power of God. His cry is the heart of the story. He acknowledged his lack of faith and looked to Jesus for help: 'I believe: help my unbelief!' (v. 34) At that moment he stood in sharp contrast to the Twelve who displayed their lack of trust. Jesus 'lifted up' one who looked like a corpse (v. 26).

Now, the disciples learned what rising from the dead meant (9:10): Christ's victory over the forces of evil. Through union with their Master in prayer they can share in that same power. Bereft of his presence, stripped of communion with him, Christians are powerless and helpless (see John 15:1-5)

2 PETER

The second letter of Peter offers a footnote on the transfiguration (2 Pet 1:16-19) This letter, written in the name of Peter, is in fact the latest New Testament writing – from about 125 A.D. In the relevant passage the author is refuting some who reject the traditional belief in the 'second coming' of Jesus – the *parousia* – as a 'cleverly devised myth'.

He counters by asserting that Christianity is no clever fable but is rooted in history, in the person of Jesus, and in the attestation of Spirit-filled witnesses. He instances the episode of the transfiguration. In his *persona* of Peter he can vouch for it: he was 'with him [Jesus] on the holy mountain' (v. 18). He interprets the event as a prediction of the *parousia*. The 'majesty' he had beheld, the divine attestation he had heard, were a glimpse and a promise of the full glory of the Beloved Son at his *parousia*. In short, we have here an interesting instance of an early Christian adaptation of the transfiguration.

5 Supper

*'As often as you eat this bread and drink the cup,
you proclaim the Lord's death until he comes.'
(1 Corinthians 11:26).*

Mark 14:12-28

¹²On the first day of Unleavened Bread, when the Passover lamb is sacrificed, his disciples said to him, 'Where do you want us to go and make the preparations for you to eat the Passover?' ¹³So he sent two of his disciples, saying to them, 'Go into the city, and a man carrying a jar of water will meet you; follow him, ¹⁴and wherever he enters, say to the owner of the house, "The Teacher asks, Where is my guest room where I may eat the Psassover with my disciples?" ¹⁵He will show you a large room upstairs, furnished and ready. Make preparations for us there.' ¹⁶So the disciples set out and went to the city, and found everything as he had told them; and they prepared the Passover meal.

¹⁷When it was evening he came with the twelve. ¹⁸And when they had taken their places and were eating, Jesus said, 'Truly I tell you, one of you will betray me, one who is eating with me. ¹⁹They began to be distressed and to say to him one after another, 'Surely, not I?' ²⁰He said to them, 'It is one of the twelve, one who is dipping bread into the bowl with me. ²¹For the Son of Man goes as it is written of him, but woe to the one by whom the Son of Man is betrayed! It would have been better for that one not to have been born.'

²²While they were eating, he took a loaf of bread, and after blessing it he broke it, gave it to them, and said, 'Take; this is my body.' ²³Then he took a cup, and after giving thanks he gave it to them, and all of them drank from it. ²⁴He said to them, 'This is my blood of the covenant, which is poured out for many. ²⁵Truly I tell you, I will never again drink of the fruit of the vine until that day when I drink it new in the kingdom of God.'

Matthew 26:20-29

²⁰When it was evening, he took his place with the twelve; ²¹and while they were eating, he said, 'Truly I tell you, one of you will betray me.' ²²And they became greatly distressed and began to say to him one after another, 'Surely not I, Lord?' ²³He answered, 'The one who has dipped his hand into the bowl with me will betray me. ²⁴The Son of Man goes as it is written of him, but woe to that one by whom the Son of Man is betrayed! It would have been better for that one not to have been born.' ²⁵Judas, who betrayed him, said, 'Surely not I, Rabbi?' He replied, 'You have said so.'

²⁶While they were eating, Jesus took a loaf of bread, and after blessing it he broke it, gave it to the disciples, and said, 'Take, eat; this is my body.' ²⁷Then he took a cup, and after giving thanks he gave it to them, saying, 'Drink from it, all of you; ²⁸for this is my blood of the covenant, which is poured out for many for the forgiveness of sins. ²⁹I tell you, I will never again drink

of this fruit of the vine until that day when I drink it new with you in my Father's kingdom.'

Luke 22:14-23

[14]When the hour came, he took his place at the table, and the apostles with him. [15]He said to them, 'I have eagerly desired to eat this Passover with you before I suffer; [16]for I tell you, I will not eat it until it is fulfilled in the kingdom of God.' [17]Then he took a cup, and after giving thanks he said, 'Take this and divide it among yourselves; [18]for I tell you that from now on I will not drink of the fruit of the vine until the kingdom of God comes.' [19]Then he took a loaf of bread, and when he had given thanks, he broke it and gave it to them, saying, 'This is my body, which is given for you. Do this in remembrance of me.' [20]And he did the same with the cup after supper, saying, 'This cup that is poured out for you is the new covenant in my blood. [21]But see, the one who betrays me is with me, and his hand is on the table. [22]For the Son of Man is going as it has been determined, but woe to that one by whom he is betrayed!. [23]Then they began to ask one another which one of them it could be who would do this.

1 Corinthians 11: 17-33

[17]Now in the following instructions I do not commend you, because when you come together it is not for the better but for the worse. [18]For, to begin with, when you come together as a church, I hear that there

are divisions among you; and to some extent I believe it. [19]Indeed, there have to be factions among you, for only so will it become clear who among you are genuine. [20]When you come together, it is not really to eat the Lord's supper. [21]For when the time comes to eat, each of you goes ahead with your own supper, and one goes hungry while another becomes drunk. [22]What! Do you not have homes to eat and drink in? Or do you show contempt for the church of God and humiliate those who have nothing? What should I say to you? Should I commend you? In this matter I do not commend you!

[23]For I received from the Lord what I also handed on to you, that the Lord Jesus on the night when he was betrayed took a loaf of bread, [24]and when he had given thanks, he broke it and said, 'This is my body that is for you. Do this in remembrance of me.' [25]In the same way he took the cup also, after supper, saying, 'This cup is the new covenant in my blood. Do this, as often as you drink it, in remembrance of me.' [26]For as often as you eat this bread and drink the cup, you proclaim the Lord's death until he comes.

[27]Whoever, therefore, eats the bread or drinks the cup of the Lord in an unworthy manner will be answerable for the body and blood of the Lord. [28]Examine yourselves, and only then eat of the bread and drink of the cup. [29]For all who eat and drink without discerning the body, eat and drink judgment against themselves. [30]For this reason many of you are weak and ill, and some have died. [31]But if we judged

oursleves, we would not be judged. [32]But when we are judged by the Lord, we are disciplined so that we may not be condemned along with the world.

[33]So then, my brothers and sisters, when you come together to eat, wait for one another. [34]If you are hungry, eat at home, so that when you come together, it will not be for your condemnation. About the other things I will give instructions when I come.

1 Corinthians 10:16-17
[16]The cup of blessing that we bless, is it not a sharing in the blood of Christ? The bread that we break, is it not a sharing in the body of Christ? [17]Because there is one bread, we who are many are one body, for we all partake of the one bread.

MARK

Mark's concern in 14:12-25 was to connect this farewell meal of Jesus with the Passover – in v. 14 he explicitly designates it a Passover meal. This means that, in his chronology, Jesus died on the feast of Passover, and in this he is followed by Matthew and Luke. The Fourth Gospel, however, has a different chronology, and states with equal clarity (John 18:28; 19:14) that Jesus died on 14 Nisan – eve of Passover.

What is essential here is that the Synoptists and John firmly link the death of Jesus with Passover: the Synoptists by having him eat the Passover meal and die on the feast; John by having him condemned to death at the hour when Passover lambs were being sacrificed.

In reality it would seem most likely that the Last Supper

was a solemn farewell meal – not a traditional Passover meal. It was the culmination of a series of meals that Jesus had shared with his disciples. Daniel Harrington observes:

> Apart from Mark 14:12-15 (Matthew 26:17-20) one would assume that Jesus' Last Supper was a regular meal with the overtones of the Passover season – something like holding a Christmas party on December 24. This schema is consistent with the plan of the high priests and elders to avoid arresting Jesus *during* the feast. They do so beforehand. [18]

What can be said without contest is that, whatever the precise nature of the Last Supper, the background for it was Passover. The evangelists exploit this factor.

The construction of the passage Mark 14:12-16 is very like that of the preparation for the entry into Jerusalem in 11:1-6 where the intent is the same. Here, as there, two disciples are sent off with a precise description of the situation they will encounter and here, too, all turned out as the Teacher had assured them. The Jesus who had perceived the sombre significance of his anointing by a woman – 'she has anointed my body beforehand for burial' (14:8) – knows that his hour has come. He goes to meet it.

'His disciples said to him' (v. 12) – the disciples were a goodly number of men and women who had left everything to accompany Jesus on his itinerant mission. The Twelve formed the symbolic core of the group. The room required for the meal is 'large' – literally, 'great' (v. 15), sug-

18. *The Gospel of Matthew*. Sacra Pagina 1. A Michael Glazier Book. (Collegeville, MN: The Liturgical Press, 1991), 370 f.

gesting that more than the Twelve and Jesus were at the Supper.

Examine yourselves

Between preparation for the Supper and the Supper itself the evangelist inserted the announcement-of-betrayal passage (vv. 17-21). Jesus' opening words (v. 18) echo Psalm 14:9: 'Even my bosom friend in whom I trusted, who ate of my bread, has lifted up his heel against me.'

The words, 'one who is eating with me … dipping bread into the dish with me,' express the horror of treachery in the sacred setting of table fellowship. There was the added awfulness: it is one of the Twelve. Shattering though it be, betrayal was in accordance with the divine plan for the passion: 'as it is written.' But human responsibility was not thereby diminished. What was written was that the Son of Man 'goes': death was accepted by Jesus himself.

Behind it all is a chastening admonishment to the reader. Mark has placed the betrayal episode in the context of eucharistic table fellowship. The Christian must ask: 'Is it I?' – am I a betrayer of the Lord Jesus?' (see v. 19). One is reminded of Paul in 1 Corinthians 11:28: 'Examine yourselves, and only then eat of the bread and drink of the cup.'

The Lord's Supper

The phrase, 'While they were eating' (Mark 14:22), not only resumes the meal episode after the warning of betrayal but, as a conscious echo of v. 18a, emphasises the betrayal warning.

Jesus followed the practice of a family head at a festive Jewish meal by breaking a loaf and passing around the pieces.

He 'took bread,' 'blessed,' 'broke,' 'gave': the same actions and the very same words as in both feeding stories (6:41; 8:6). There is no doubt that the correspondence is intentional; the vocabulary there was prompted by the eucharistic language here. Then, the disciples 'did not understand about the loaves' (6:52; see 8:17-21); now, the mystery is being revealed. Jesus is the 'one loaf' (see 8:14) for Jews and Gentiles because, as he tells them, his body is being given and his blood poured out for all (14:23-24).

'This is my body' (14:22): Paul (1 Corinthians 11:22) adds 'which is for you.' But this is firmly implied in Mark both through repeated references to Jesus' death since the beginning of the passion narrative and the explicit statement over the cup: 'This is my blood of the covenant' (Mark 14:24). Moses' words at the sealing of the Sinai covenant (Exodus 24:8) are certainly in mind: 'See the blood of the covenant that the Lord has made with you.' By the sprinkling of sacrificial blood the people of Israel shared in the blessings of the covenant given at Sinai. Likewise, this blood of the cup 'will be poured out' (a future nuance) 'for many' (a semitism, meaning 'all'): a new covenant is being forged and sealed whose blessings are offered to all (Mark 14:24). In giving his 'body and blood' Jesus is giving his very self and giving it in death. The death of Jesus is always 'for' others (see Galatians 2:20; Romans 5:8; 8:32). The Last Supper helps us to understand the meaning of Jesus' death on Calvary.

The saying of Mark 14:25 – 'Truly I tell you, I will never again drink of the fruit of the vine until that day when I drink it new in the kingdom of God' – is likely to have been, in some form, part of Mark's liturgical tradition. It is, in essence, quite like the declaration in 1 Corinthians 11:26: 'For as often as you eat this bread and drink the cup, you proclaim the Lord's death until he comes.' As it stands in the Supper narrative, Jesus looks forward, beyond death, to the kingdom. As in the predictions of the passion (8:31; 9:31; 10:33-34) death is not the last word. Here Jesus looks, with sure hope, to the eschatological banquet.

His words also suggest a break: the close association, supremely marked by table fellowship, with his disciples, was at an end. But by expressing to them his own serene expectation, he was assuring them of renewed communion in the kingdom. This point has been made explicitly by Matthew (26:29). John Donahue has an enlightening comment on the actualizing of the Marcan Last Supper:

> Vatican II provided an excellent guideline for proper interpretation by speaking of the 'twofold table of the Lord's Word and of the Supper.' In Markan terms this means that it is the Jesus of the gospel, God's chosen prophet and suffering servant, who gives his life for many. It also means that reception of the Eucharist cannot be separated from responding to the challenge of discipleship that permeates the gospel, though the failure of the chosen Twelve serves as a warning that meeting this challenge is never complete. As a covenant 'in my blood' the Eucharist is a promise that Jesus will be with the believer in the present and in the future banquet of the kingdom. [19]

19. John R. Donahue and Daniel J. Harrington, *The Gospel of Mark*. Sacra Pagina 2. A Michael Glazier Book. (Collegeville, MN: The Liturgical Press, 2002), 400.

MATTHEW

Matthew's account (26:26-29) of Jesus' Last Supper follows Mark very closely. He has, however, made one notable addition: 'This is my blood of the covenant, which is poured out for many *for the forgiveness of sins*.' (26:28) Matthew alone, in the New Testament Last Supper accounts, refers to the forgiveness of sins. Jesus' power to forgive sins is a distinctive emphasis of this evangelist (see 1:21; 5:23-24; 6:12-15; 9:6; 18:21-35).

LUKE

In some New Testament manuscripts verses 19b-20 of Luke's Last Supper narrative (22:14-20) are omitted. The presence of two cups (vv 17,20) over which Jesus had pronounced a blessing had disconcerted some copyists. To judge from the manuscript evidence, the first cup was regarded as being sufficiently eucharistic and the other was set aside. It is also likely that the words of v. 17 were closer to the liturgical formula which was familiar to the scribes in question.

The longer reading is, today, readily accepted. Luke has emphasised that, for him, the Last Supper was a Passover meal. There were four successive cups of wine at Passover, each with its own blessing. Luke's two cups would reflect that practice.

Luke has the command: 'Do this in remembrance of me'. (v. 19) The term 'remembrance' (*anamnesis*) means 'to bring to mind' – but a bringing to mind that is a form of presence.

As the bread must be broken to be shared, so is his body to be broken in death so that the life-giving spirit might be given to them. When they [the disciples (and readers)] in turn 'do this as a remembrance of him' in their 'breaking bread' together (Acts 2:46; 20:7), he will be present not as a fond memory but as a powerful and commanding presence. [20]

What is to be 'remembered' is Jesus himself.

PAUL (1 CORINTHIANS 10:16-17; 11:17-34)

Apart from two passages in 1 Corinthians it might have seemed that Paul knew nothing of the Eucharist — surely a salutary reminder that what we have from Paul are occasional letters by no means giving his whole theology or the full content of his preaching. At any rate, 1 Corinthians 11:23-26 puts beyond doubt that the Lord's Supper had been part of Christian faith and practice from the start. The passage is the earliest reference in the New Testament to the Eucharist:

> [23]For I received from the Lord what I also handed on to you, that the Lord Jesus on the night when he was betrayed took a loaf of bread, [24]and when he had given thanks, he broke it and said, 'This is my body that is for you. Do this in remembrance of me.' [25]In the same way he took the cup also, after supper, saying, 'This cup is the new covenant in my blood. Do this, as often as you drink it, in remembrance of me.' [26]For as often as you eat this bread and drink the cup, you proclaim the Lord's death until he comes.

20. Luke Timothy Johnson, *The Gospel of Luke*. Sacra Pagina 3. A Michael Glazier Book (Collegeville, MN: The Liturgical Press, 1991), 342.

Paul solemnly passes on a tradition which, because it reached him through an authentically Christian community, had come to him from 'the Lord'. In fact, he is citing an established liturgical text – likely the usage of the church of Antioch. [21] He reminds the Corinthians of this tradition in the course of correcting an abuse in their celebration (11:17-22).

The striking point in the passage (11:23-26) is that Paul does not think of the Eucharist and Christ's presence in a static manner as might be suggested by the formulas 'This is ... '. Instead, the account is full of dynamic expressions. It is no mere making present of Christ's body and blood; it is a proclamation, and a memorial of his death, of an event. Similarly, the cup is 'the new covenant in my blood,' that is, an event, the making of a covenant that has lasting and definitive consequences for the life of the people who are included in the covenant.

The command to repeat the action of the Lord, 'Do this ... ', not only binds the community to celebrate the Lord's Supper regularly and thus keep alive the meaning of the death of Jesus, but places upon it the obligation to proclaim the redemptive meaning of his death.

'Do this in remembrance of me': Paul wants to evoke an active remembrance that would make the past present by recall of total commitment to Christ. Significantly, the 'proclamation' of the Lord's death is in terms of an eating and drinking that implies a true communion – for nothing but

21. All four texts (the Synoptists and Paul) of the Last Supper ritual are liturgical. They may be reduced to two: Paul/Luke and Mark/Matthew.

love, expressed in warm table fellowship, can continue to proclaim the meaning of the death of Christ.

Sharing

Just here lay the Corinthian problem. The Eucharist was celebrated in the setting of a community meal. At Corinth it had become fashionable for the better-off members of the community to gather beforehand and dine well on their lavish provision of food and drink. Later, when the workers and slaves turned up, the Eucharist was celebrated (11:17-22, 33-34). Or, at least, these 'second-class' members had to be content with simpler fare.

In Paul's eyes this was not only a glaring abuse but a perversion of the whole meaning and purpose of the Lord's Supper. He had declared: 'The cup of blessing that we bless, is it not a sharing in the blood of Christ? The bread that we break, is it not a sharing in the body of Christ?' (10:16). His emphasis was not just on the one bread and the one cup but on the *sharing* of the one loaf and the one cup. It is because, in sharing mode, they partake of the one loaf, that the celebrants become 'one body' – the Body of Christ. 'Because there is one bread, we who are many are one body, for we all partake of the one bread' (10:17). The Eucharist was meant to be a bond of unity; in Corinth it had been turned into a wedge between the haves and the have-nots. No wonder that Paul does not commend the Corinthian practice (11:17, 22).

Because this context is ignored, v. 29 has been regularly misinterpreted – 'For all who eat and drink without discerning the body, eat and drink judgment against themselves.' Traditionally, the verse has been urged in support of the doctrine of the real presence — the sin being that one fails to distinguish the Eucharist from ordinary food and drink. In point of fact, the 'real presence' is not an issue; the Corinthians do believe that they are eating and drinking 'the body and blood of the Lord'. (11:27) The point at issue is that what was designed to unify is being used to divide. The 'body' in question in v. 29 is *the body of the community* (the Body of Christ). The Corinthian celebration is not communion. The sacrament of the body and blood of the Lord is being abused to rend the body of Christ.

Paul goes further: 'When you come together, it is not really to eat the Lord's Supper'. (11:20) A Lord's Supper that was not a shared supper, that was not a *sharing* in the one bread and in the one cup, was not *in fact* the Lord's Supper. Even though the ritual words (vv. 24-25) were said, the lack of love (vv. 21-22) meant that in reality there was no Eucharist. The essence of Paul's reaction is that there can be no Eucharist in a community whose members do not love one another.

This must surely give food for thought. To what extent is our Mass truly a celebration of the Lord's Supper? [22]

22. This is an issue of current concern. Siobhán Garrigan, Assistant Professor of Liturgical Studies at Yale Divinity School, observes at the conclusion of an article on Roman Catholic eucharistic practice: 'Not until we eat real bread in our liturgies will we make the connection between Jesus' message in the gospels and the terrible hunger in the world. Not until we drink real wine will we get a taste of the realm we are called to co-create with God. Not until we drink from a single cup and eat from a whole loaf will we feel that extraordinary unity of love (based on forgiveness) God calls us to believe in. Not until we feel we have shared a meal will we notice who is absent. Not until we have

JOHN

John 13:1-35

¹Now before the festival of the passover, Jesus knew that his hour had come to depart from the world and go to the Father. Having loved his own who were in the world, he loved them to the end. ²The devil had already put it into the heart of Judas son of Simon Iscariot to betray him. And during supper ³Jesus, knowing that the Father had given all things into his hands, and that he had come from God and was going to God, ⁴got up from the table, took off his outer robe, and tied a towel around himself. ⁵Then he poured water into a basin and began to wash the disciples' feet and to wipe them with the towel that was tied around him. ⁶He came to Simon Peter, who said to him, 'Lord, are you going to wash my feet?' ⁷Jesus answered, 'You do not know what I am doing, but later you will understand.' ⁸Peter said to him, 'You will never wash my feet.' Jesus answered, 'Unless I wash you, you have no share with me.' ⁹Simon Peter

---

bought and held and offered and blessed and shared and consumed the food and drink ourselves, and cleaned up afterwards, will we be able to talk about the leadership or 'priesthood' we need for the future. And maybe if we admit that what we are doing at the moment is just a string of paltry substitutions, we will understand why our children make their Holy Communion for the money and only drop back in on their wedding day, when they get to taste the wine.' ('Eat and Drink – All of You,' *The Furrow* 53, November 2002), 610. In similar vein see Thomas O'Loughlin, 'Breaking and Sharing: Inspiration from Early Christian Ireland', (*Scripture in Church* 31, April-June 2001), 246-249.

said to him, 'Lord, not my feet only but also my hands and my head!' ¹⁰Jesus said to him, 'One who has bathed does not need to wash, except for the feet, but is entirely clean, though not all of you.' ¹¹For he knew who was to betray him; for this reason, he said, 'Not all of you are clean.'

¹²After he had washed their feet, had put on his robe, and had returned to the table, he said to them, 'Do you know what I have done to you? ¹³You call me Teacher and Lord – and you are right, for that is what I am. ¹⁴So if I, your Lord and Teacher, have washed your feet, you also ought to wash one another's feet. ¹⁵For I have set you an example, that you also should do as I have done to you. ¹⁶Very truly, I tell you, servants are not greater than their master, nor are messengers greater than the one who sent them. ¹⁷If you know these things, you are blessed if you do them. ¹⁸I am not speaking of all of you; I know whom I have chosen. But it is to fulfil the scripture, 'the one who ate my bread has lifted his heel against me.' ¹⁹I tell you this now, before it occurs, so that when it does occur, you may believe that I AM. ²⁰Very truly, I tell you, whoever receives one whom I send receives me; and whoever receives me receives him who sent me.

²¹After saying this Jesus was troubled in spirit, and declared, 'Very truly, I tell you, one of you will betray me.' ²²The disciples looked at one another, uncertain of whom he was speaking. ²³One of his disciples – the one whom Jesus loved – was reclining next to him. ²⁴Simon Peter therefore motioned to him to ask Jesus

of whom he was speaking. [25]So while reclining next to Jesus, he asked him, 'Lord, who is it?' [26]Jesus answered, 'It is the one to whom I give this piece of bread when I have dipped it in the dish.' So when he had dipped the piece of bread, [he took it and] he gave it to Judas son of Simon Iscariot. [27]After he had received the piece of bread, Satan entered into him. Jesus said to him, 'Do quickly what you are going to do.' [28]Now no one at the table knew why he said this to him. [29]Some thought that because Judas had the common purse, Jesus was telling him, 'Buy what we need for the festival;' or, that he should give something to the poor. [30]So, after receiving the piece of bread, he immediately went out. And it was night.

[31]When he had gone out, Jesus said, 'Now the Son of Man has been glorified, and God has been glorified in him. [32]If God has been glorified in him, God will also glorify him in himself and will glorify him at once. [33]Little children, I am with you only a little longer. You will look for me; and as I said to the Jews so now I say to you, 'Where I am going. you cannot come.' [34]I gave you a new commandment, that you love one another. Just as I have loved you, you also should love one another. [35]By this everyone will know that you are my disciples, if you have love for one another.'

The Supper narrative of the Fourth Gospel does not include an account of the institution of the Eucharist. The Eucharist, however, is surely in the background, and John's understanding of its significance for Christians is quite like that of Paul.

The 'hour' had come (13:1). Before departing, Jesus would tell his disciples, in a manner they could never forget, how utterly he loved them. Jesus knew that he was about to give the supreme manifestation (see 15:13) of his abiding love for his disciples. He himself brought out clearly the meaning of what he did, the act of humble service he now rendered.

The opening words (13:1) are a caption for all that is to come in chapters 13-17, the demonstration of Jesus' love for his own – a love to the end (*eis telos*), without measure: 'Having loved his own who were in the world, he loved them to the end (he loved them utterly).'

Jesus laid aside his garments (13:4,12) as he had spoken of laying down his life (10:18). The disciples were to have a 'share' with him (13:8); the washing of feet expressed symbolically that they are brought into communion of life with Jesus through his death, a supreme act of self-giving and humble service. It is necessary to be washed by Jesus, giver of life, if one is to have part with him in eternal life – one must share in his death and resurrection. Baptism is surely in the background. One is reminded of Paul's rhetorical question: 'Do you not know that all of us who have been baptized into Christ Jesus were baptized into his death?' (Romans 6:3)

I have washed your feet

'I have set you an example.' The disciples are not to look only to his ultimate gesture of love; humble service should characterise all the living of his followers. Here is a moving lesson in *diakonia*. Jesus is indeed Lord and Teacher; he has authority. But his style and exercise of authority are marked by service. The whole of Jesus' life, culminating in his death and resurrection, was a passage from 'this world' to the Father, from death to life, for us.

'That you may believe that I AM' (v. 19). He had spoken of his betrayal. He cannot mean that the betrayal as such would reveal Jesus as bearer of the divine name and power. He meant that the betrayal, the 'delivering up,' would trigger the procedure that would lead to his 'lifting up' and his revelation of himself and of the Father (see 8:28). The reality which Christ gives us is himself as the 'one for others'. If we really receive him as such we must ourselves become 'people for others,' servants of our fellows. Our challenge is our ongoing 'passage' from selfishness to service (vv. 1-20).

Jesus had set an example (v. 15). He knew that his example would be ignored. Those who, down the ages, will claim to speak in his name would, too often, speak with arrogant self-assurance. He would, over and over, be betrayed. Jesus' awareness of future betrayal was focused, here and now, on the presence of a traitor at his farewell supper. He declared, 'One of you will betray me.' A favourite disciple, not one of the twelve, who reclined by him, asked who that person was. Jesus told him, quietly, that it was the one to whom he would hand a morsel of bread he had dipped in the common dish. 'When he had dipped the morsel he took it and gave it to Judas' (13:26).

Hereby hangs a tale. Some early manuscripts of the Fourth Gospel omit 'he took it' – it is not in the NRSV, the version I follow; it ought to be! That Jesus 'took bread' occurs in all the Gospel feeding stories and in the Synoptic and Pauline Last Supper accounts. The phrase, to Christian ears, has unmistakable eucharistic overtones. Francis Moloney's comment is splendidly perceptive:

> Scribes could not tolerate the idea that the sharing of the morsel between Jesus and Judas might have eucharistic overtones and thus they eliminated words that made the association explicit. Just as baptism is a sub-theme to the foot-washing, Eucharist is a sub-theme to the meal and the gift of the morsel. Within the context of a meal, indicated as eucharistic, Jesus gives the morsel to the most despised character in the Johannine narrative: Judas. Disciples always have and always will display ignorance, fail Jesus, and deny him. Some may even betray him in an outrageous and public way. But Jesus' never-failing love for such disciples, a love that reached out even to the archetype of the evil disciple, reveals a unique God (cf vv 18-20). This is what it means to love *eis telos* (v 1). [23]

A new commandment

Jesus had assured his own of how wholly he loved them. He would now speak to them his last will and testament. The betrayer had gone to his task. For him 'it was night' (v. 30) – he had turned his back on the light of the world. But he had not escaped the care of the shepherd (vv. 21-30). Jesus was alone with his own disciples. In our text, the general context is that of Eucharist which, though never explicitly mentioned, is implicit throughout.

'Now the Son of Man has been glorified'. (v. 31) The 'now' is the hour of decision and consummation, belong-

23. Francis J. Moloney, *op. cit.*, 384.

ing in time, yet decisive for eternity. Now, by going forward to the cross, by being 'lifted up,' Jesus is about to achieve his 'glory' – his revelation of his loving Father. Already he had told 'the Jews': 'where I am going you cannot come' (7:34; 8:21-22). But the reason on that occasion was their 'sin.' Here the separation from the disciples is occasioned by his death. While they cannot come to him, he will come to them.

In the meantime they will live with this new 'commandment'. The 'newness' here is the newness of the covenant and is perpetuated in the Eucharist. What is new in this covenant is love 'as I have loved you'. Even if Jesus departs and they cannot now follow him to the Father, they can still be 'followers' of Jesus here and now, and they can keep his spirit alive among themselves (vv. 34-35). As long as they keep true to the 'new commandment,' as long as Christian love is in this world (the 'Christian' love, too, of many who do not know him), the world still encounters Jesus.

Conclusion

What has come into being in him was life,
and the life was the light of all people ...
I am the light of the world.
(John 1:4; 8:12).

The Mysteries of Light reveal the Light that is light of the world, that is life of the world. They reveal the incarnate Word: Jesus of Nazareth. The Rosary is, in essence, a meditation on the Son of Mary, the one who is the revelation and the presence of God. Paul has assured us: 'God was in Christ, reconciling the world to himself'. (2 Corinthians 5:19) In Jesus, God has revealed himself as Parent. Through the Spirit of the risen Jesus, God has assured us of our filial status: 'When we cry "Abba! Father!" it is that very Spirit bearing witness with our spirit that we are children of God, and if children, then heirs, heirs of God and joint heirs with Christ' (Romans 8:15-17). Joint heirs with Christ – he is our elder Brother. We would know him better. And knowing him will lead us to knowledge of our Parent, for the Son is 'the reflection of God's glory and the exact imprint of God's very being' (Hebrews 1:3).

Here we summarise what we have seen in the Mysteries.

BAPTISM

His baptism by John the Baptist marked the start of the short active ministry of Jesus of Nazareth. He began as disciple of John but, before long, launched his own distinctive mission. His goal was the renewal of Israel: to bring Israel to what God had wanted his people to be. At the Baptism

Jesus was solemnly proclaimed Son of God: leader of God's End-time people – Lord of his people.

Jesus was Son of God, yet like his brothers and sisters in every respect. He was tested – he had to make decisions throughout his life. Being Son did not spare him: 'Although he was Son, he learned obedience through what he suffered'. (Hebrews 5:8) He had learned how costly saying Yes to God might be: his Yes led him to the Cross. Paul had found inspiration and comfort in the faith of Jesus: 'The life I now live in the flesh I live by the faith of the Son of God, who loved me and gave himself for me'. (Galatians 2:20) The faithful Son is our support in our testing.

CANA

'The law indeed was given through Moses, grace and truth came through Jesus Christ.' (John 1:17) The revelation of God that is Torah was, indeed, gift, *charis*. The 'truth,' the fulness of revelation, is in the Son. Cana marked the first moment of 'glory', *doxa* – that definitive revelation. The fullness of revelation would be when the Son of Man was 'lifted up.' He was the Sent One who spoke the I AM of the Father's presence and authority. He spoke that Word on the Cross.

'And blessed is she who believed' (Luke 1:45) – Elizabeth had pinpointed the characteristic trait of Mary in the Gospels: she is the woman of faith. This is especially so in the Fourth Gospel. At Cana she herself exemplified, and then demanded, total trust in the word of her Son. She becomes the example for Christians and Advocate for her Son. She points beyond herself. In her fashion she endorses the dec-

laration of the Son: 'I am the vine, you are the branches …
Apart from me you can do nothing.' (John 15:5) She continues to admonish us: 'Do whatever he tells you.' (2:5)

Her ongoing role was confirmed at 'the hour' of her Son.
She and the Beloved Disciple are, in John's theology, the
believers *par excellence*. They are the nucleus of a new family of believers. They had been witnesses of 'the hour': the
definitive revelation of God. Now they must bear witness.
The Beloved Disciple had seen the truth and had believed
before any encounter with the risen Lord (20:8). He was
the model of future believers: 'Blessed are those who have
not seen and yet have come to believe.' (20:29) The Mother
had been told, 'Here is your Son.' (19:26) Become mother
of the Beloved Disciple, she is, thereby, mother of all Christians. The fourth evangelist's creative imagination is vehicle
of his rich theology.

KINGDOM

The basic sense of 'kingdom of God,' as understood and
meant by Jesus, was the End-time rule of God when, as
Paul put it, God will be 'all in all' (1 Corinthians 15:28).
Then will the prayer of Jesus be fulfilled: 'Your kingdom
come. Your will be done on earth as it is in heaven.' (Matthew 5:10) Jesus, however, had insisted that, in his person
ansd ministry, the rule of God had become a reality here
and now. In the words of Ambrose: 'Life means living with
Christ. Where Christ is, there too is life and there is the
kingdom.' (*Vita est enim esse cum Christo; ergo, ubi Christus,
ibi vita, ibi regnum.*)

In his proclamation of the Kingdom, Jesus' presupposition was God as Parent – with humankind, God's children, as brothers and sisters. This is why he stood authority on its head. Because the community of his followers should be marked by fellowship, *koinonia*, the pattern of dominion should have no place: 'it is not so among you.' (Mark 10:43) Authority finds its expression in *service*.

In a world of stark inequality and injustice, Jesus had particular concern for the afflicted, the marginalised. 'Outcast' was not a category he would or could acknowledge. He displayed notable respect for women and children. He was sensitive to suffering and was prodigal in healing the ills of humankind. He had special concern for the destructive illness that is sin – so much so that he was known as 'friend of sinners.'

Himself Torah-observant, Jesus was sharply critical of religion. He set aside a 'tradition of the elders' that, too readily, conflicted with the spirit of God's will for humankind: 'You abandon the commandment of God and hold to human tradition.' (Mark 7:8) His attitude is summed up in one pithy and challenging declaration: 'The sabbath was made for humankind, not humankind for the sabbath.' (2:27)

As the Sent One of the Father, Jesus was a man of prayer, an inspiration to his followers. Following him was no soft option: his men and women disciples had left everything. His own way led to the Cross: 'No one has greater love than this, to lay down one's life for one's friend.' (John 15:13). The rule of God is a way of love.

TRANSFIGURATION

The transfiguration was, very likely, a prayer experience in which Jesus came to terms with his 'departure': his death, his *exodos*. Evidently, the experience was so profound that it left an indelible impression on disciples who had witnessed it. Viewed in retrospect, in the light of the resurrection, it was taken to have been an anticipated glimpse of Jesus in glory. Now it is recast as an episode for the benefit of the disciples, a revelation granted to them. And the climax is the word from heaven: 'This is my Son, the Beloved; listen to him.' (Mark 9:7)

In Matthew's version the disciples, overcome by fear, were reassured by Jesus: 'And when they looked up, they saw no one except Jesus himself alone.' (Matthew 17:8)

Moses and Elijah still speak words of God, but not the definitive word. Now is 'the gift in place of a gift.' (John 1:16) Now God 'has spoken to us by a Son.' (Hebrews 1:2) We, like the father of the epileptic boy, pray to the Son to aid our lack of faith. United with him in prayer, we are no longer helpless. We can share the experience of Paul: 'I can do all things through him who strengthens me.' (Philippians 4:13)

SUPPER

'This is my body … this is my blood.' By speaking of 'body and blood', that is to say, the self, the person, Jesus is giving himself, and giving himself in death. Paul had grasped the significance of the gift – gift of 'the Son of God, who loved me and gave himself for me'. (Galatians 1:20) The death of Jesus is 'for' us.

'You proclaim the death of the Lord': the Supper is the interpretation of the death of Jesus. The Eucharist is *anamnesis*: a bringing to mind that is a form of presence. The Eucharist fulfils the promise of the risen Lord: 'Remember, I am with you always, to the end of the age.' (Matthew 28:20)

'We who are many are one body': the Eucharist is meant to be a bond of unity . Eucharistic Celebration ought to be a manifest witness to unity. Paul's view that, where this is not so there is in fact no Eucharist, should make us ponder. Is our Eucharistic Celebration, our Mass, a manifest sign of unity? Is it, truly, the Lord's Supper? Salutary indeed – but one would close on a positive note. [24]

The Book of Revelation is markedly liturgical. It is explicitly designated for reading in a liturgy (1:3), very likely a Eucharistic Liturgy. It closes with a look to the One who is coming soon, 'bringing his reward with him'. (22:12) Christians, if they were faithful, would share his triumph. They look for his coming.

In the meantime, as they celebrate their Eucharist, they have his presence with them. They have the reminder of his victory and the assurance of his presence: 'As often as you eat this bread and drink the cup, you proclaim the Lord's death until he comes.' (1 Corinthians 11:26) They did not have to wait, bereft, for his final coming.

Yet, they long. 'My desire is to depart and be with Christ, for that is far better.' (Philippians 1:23) It is in their going to him that the Lord will come to them – and to us! *Maranatha.*

24. Wilfrid J. Harrington, *Seeking Spiritual Growth Through the Bible* (New York: Paulist Press, 2002), 94-95.

CONCLUSION

Come, Lord Jesus! Perhaps in our Eucharistic Celebration we might capture something of this assurance and this hope.